New Directions for
Community Colleges

Arthur M. Cohen
EDITOR-IN-CHIEF

Caroline Q. Durdella
Nathan R. Durdella
ASSOCIATE EDITORS

Amy Fara Edwards
MANAGING EDITOR

D0746938

Budget and Finance in the American Community College

Trudy H. Bers
Ronald B. Head
James C. Palmer

EDITORS

Number 168 • Winter 2014
Jossey-Bass
San Francisco

BUDGET AND FINANCE IN THE AMERICAN COMMUNITY COLLEGE
Trudy H. Bers, Ronald B. Head, James C. Palmer (eds.)
New Directions for Community Colleges, no. 168

Arthur M. Cohen, Editor-in-Chief
Caroline Q. Durdella, Nathan R. Durdella, Associate Editors
Amy Fara Edwards, Managing Editor

NEW DIRECTIONS FOR COMMUNITY COLLEGES (ISSN 0194-3081, electronic ISSN 1536-0733) is part of The Jossey-Bass Higher and Adult Education Series and is published quarterly by Wiley Subscription Services, Inc., A Wiley Company, at Jossey-Bass, One Montgomery St., Ste. 1200, San Francisco, CA 94104. POSTMASTER: Send address changes to New Directions for Community Colleges, Jossey-Bass, One Montgomery St., Ste. 1200, San Francisco, CA 94104.

SUBSCRIPTIONS cost $89 for individuals in the U.S., Canada, and Mexico, and $113 in the rest of the world for print only; $89 in all regions for electronic only; $98 in the U.S., Canada, and Mexico for combined print and electronic; $122 for combined print and electronic in the rest of the world. Institutional print only subscriptions are $335 in the U.S., $375 in Canada and Mexico, and $409 in the rest of the world; electronic only subscriptions are $335 in all regions; combined print and electronic subscriptions are $402 in the U.S., $442 in Canada and Mexico, and $476 in the rest of the world.

Cover design: Wiley
Cover Images: © Lava 4 images | Shutterstock

EDITORIAL CORRESPONDENCE should be sent to the Editor-in-Chief, Arthur M. Cohen, at 1749 Mandeville Lane, Los Angeles, CA 90049. All manuscripts receive anonymous reviews by external referees.

New Directions for Community Colleges is indexed in CIJE: Current Index to Journals in Education (ERIC), Contents Pages in Education (T&F), Current Abstracts (EBSCO), Ed/Net (Simpson Communications), Education Index/Abstracts (H. W. Wilson), Educational Research Abstracts Online (T&F), ERIC Database (Education Resources Information Center), and Resources in Education (ERIC).

Microfilm copies of issues and articles are available in 16mm and 35mm, as well as microfiche in 105mm, through University Microfilms Inc., 300 North Zeeb Road, Ann Arbor, MI 48106-1346.

CONTENTS

Editors' Notes

This *New Directions* volume is intended to fill a gap in the literature of community college finance. It was triggered by two simultaneous initiatives. First, two of the coeditors, Trudy H. Bers and Ronald B. Head, were developing materials for a course on community college effectiveness for the University of Maryland University College's doctoral program in community college policy and administration. Second, James C. Palmer, the other editor, who has long conducted research about community college finances, had recently completed a chapter on state fiscal support for community colleges for a book published in 2012 (Palmer, 2012). All three found the literature on this topic to be surprisingly sparse and dated, not fully addressing the contemporary challenge of meeting growing demands for increased student persistence and success while at the same time adjusting to such emerging issues as diminishing state support for higher education, new calls for accountability, measuring institutional effectiveness, the increasing reliance of many community colleges on grants and other sources of revenue, and college policies that have significant financial ramifications.

The three editors came together to discuss (and bemoan) the absence of current studies on community college budgets and finance and the challenge of locating substantive materials about this subject to provide to their graduate students. They decided to join together to coedit a *New Directions for Community Colleges* volume, asking their chapter authors to delve into the literature about their respective topics and to take the perspective of scholar–practitioners who would both use the literature to inform their chapters and present readers with information derived from practice.

We acknowledge that interest in community college budget and finance seems to be growing, as evidenced by a recent (July 2014) search of databases and doctoral dissertations, using the search strings "community college AND finance" and "community college AND budget." The searches resulted in a surprisingly large number of resources; for example, 827 articles in peer-reviewed journals from 2010 on, using the search string "community college AND budget." Many publications are on narrowly defined topics within these broader subject areas or are descriptive studies of individual colleges or states. Suitable as sources for in-depth literature reviews and background research for dissertations, they do not provide a readily accessible overview of key budget and finance issues for a practitioner as well as a scholarly audience. Hence, we are confident this *New Directions* fills a gap in the literature.

New Directions for Community Colleges, no. 168, Winter 2014 © 2014 Wiley Periodicals, Inc.
Published online in Wiley Online Library (wileyonlinelibrary.com) • DOI: 10.1002/cc.20115

In the first chapter, Daniel J. Phelan, president of Jackson College in Michigan, provides a discussion of major changes in community college funding that have occurred in the past decade, notably shifts away from state funding and a growing reliance on tuition without corresponding increases in student financial aid. He notes that at the same time colleges have faced intense demands to increase student retention and completion rates. His chapter traces the history of community college funding leading to the present crisis and describes its impact on the open-access mission of the community college and on the work and responsibilities of college leaders as they attempt to balance the growing demands made on their institutions and diminished public subsidies.

In Chapter 2, David S. Murphy and Stephen G. Katsinas provide practical descriptions of the basic concepts involved in budgeting and financial resources, including typical sources of revenues and expenditures; creating and balancing budgets; allocating financial resources; and meeting local, state, federal, and accrediting financial requirements. The two recognize that budgeting and managing finances often seem to be arcane processes left to the purview of chief financial officers and their staffs, yet institutional leaders in all domains need to have a basic understanding, if not day-to-day responsibility, of these critical tasks.

Palmer continues the discussion of budgets in the third chapter, summarizing the underlying assumptions and weaknesses of budgeting approaches undertaken since the 1970s, including incremental budgeting, formula budgeting, zero-base budgeting, and responsibility-center budgeting. Palmer notes the strengths of the enduring incremental approach as a way of linking resources to institutional priorities, and he points to the need for further research on how college leaders actually employ budgeting techniques to engage the campus community in making resource allocation decisions that sustain curricular continuity while at the same time adjusting funding streams to meet emerging demands for new programs and services.

Moving from the institutional to the programmatic level, Manning and Crosta, in the fourth chapter, argue that colleges need to know the financial implications of what are often perceived as routine decisions: course scheduling, program offerings, and the provision of support services. They present a methodology for estimating the cost of instructional programs for completers who follow the program's curriculum (program cost) and for students who follow a different trajectory, often not even completing a program (pathway cost). Together these measures provide important insights to guide decision makers, often revealing that programs thought to be high cost really aren't, and conversely, programs thought to be less expensive are actually more costly to the institution than commonly perceived.

A variety of policies and practices, including those developed by local boards and administrations, as well as those mandated by state and federal governments, affect budgets and finances at community colleges. Examples include tuition policies, fee structures, performance-based funding, and personnel policies. In Chapter 5, Dowd and Shieh explore some of the reasons for policy changes and provide a framework for incorporating effectiveness into the community college mission, thereby avoiding unintended negative consequences for students or the fiscal viability of the institution.

Saunders also looks at budget and finance from an institutional perspective, exploring in Chapter 6 the relationship between strategic planning and resource planning and budgeting. She describes how community college leaders can use strategic and foundational plans (academic, facilities, technology, and financial plans) to drive budgets and resource allocations in support of institutional goals and objectives. She also identifies challenges of doing so and the usefulness of budget decision packages as a way of determining the link between resource allocation decisions and the achievement of planning goals.

Focusing on revenue generation, Drummer and Marshburn in Chapter 7 look at philanthropy and private foundations as resources for expanding community colleges' revenue. They note that private funders are beginning to influence college programming, and discuss private foundations such as the Lumina Foundation for Education and the Bill and Melinda Gates Foundation, which are providing revenue tied to specific directions and prescriptions for practice. Chapter 7 also explores untapped revenue potentials and the role of local college foundations and alumni in contributing resources to community colleges.

Continuing the exploration of revenue generation strategies, Cejda and Jolley present a model of entrepreneurial waves in Chapter 8, with a special focus on the *third wave* of entrepreneurial ventures: alternative means of funding programs and services in light of continued reductions in public financial support. This third wave provides a pragmatic approach to building strong and sustainable relationships with external constituencies. Cejda and Jolley also explore the leadership characteristics necessary to create and sustain a culture of entrepreneurship.

Acknowledging the growing demand for accountability and evidence that an institution is effective in all aspects of its work, Bers and Head describe the challenge of effectively assessing community college financial services and budgets in Chapter 9. They also discuss internal and external standards and benchmarks developed to measure institutional financial health and the allocation of resources (e.g., reserve fund amounts, deferred maintenance, bond ratings).

Recognizing that the fiscal landscape for community colleges is rapidly changing, Mullin explores a number of recent innovations and trends in Chapter 10 that have emerged with respect to community college finances. He discusses performance-based funding, changes in student and institutional eligibility for financial aid, changes in local funding, generating revenue from institutional data, and the potential financial impact of massive open online courses. Mullin notes that these and other changes place new demands on community colleges and require more skilled financial managers and entrepreneurs.

Finally, Palmer pulls the volume together with concluding thoughts, synthesizing main messages and themes from the chapter and offering ideas about what lies ahead for community college budgets and finance.

Trudy H. Bers
Ronald B. Head
James C. Palmer
Editors

Reference

Palmer, J. C. (2012). State fiscal support for community colleges. In J. S. Levin & S. T. Kater (Eds.), *Understanding community colleges: Core concepts* (pp. 171–183). New York, NY: Routledge.

TRUDY H. BERS *is the president of the Bers Group, an educational consulting company, and an adjunct professor at the University of Maryland University College, Adelphi, MD.*

RONALD B. HEAD *is a professor and an assistant chair of the Doctor of Management Program in Community College Leadership and Policy at the University of Maryland University College, Adelphi, MD.*

JAMES C. PALMER *is a professor in the Department of Educational Administration and Foundations at Illinois State University, Normal, IL.*

1

This chapter describes the impact of major changes in community college funding on its open-access mission, as well as on the work and responsibilities of college leaders as they attempt to balance the increasing demands made of their institutions while concomitantly grappling with diminished public fiscal support.

The Clear and Present Funding Crisis in Community Colleges

Daniel J. Phelan

What constitutes a crisis? It's generally understood that a crisis is a troubling or dangerous situation that requires action to avoid impending or present doom, calamity, or some other undesirable circumstance. Interestingly, our ability to perceive an impending crisis seems somewhat easier when it does not directly affect us, but it seems nearly impossible to discern the threat when it's in our wheelhouse. In a now classic example of an organization that refused to recognize and act upon a looming crisis, Kaplan (2012) recounted the history of the now extinct Blockbuster Video organization, which provided quick, low-cost, and easy access to movies at outlet stores. Blockbuster executives were confident in the organization's market dominance and its reach to neighborhoods through their iconic brick-and-mortar investments on street corners throughout the country. But newcomer Netflix introduced a novel business model into the market, at first leveraging the U.S. Postal System by mailing DVDs directly to consumers, and later, making movies available through the Internet. Blockbuster did not initially recognize the disruption of this new business model, but when it began to experience a notable loss in market share, Blockbuster started paying attention, though by then it was too late to stop the fall. The company had overestimated its competitive position, failed to see the changing needs of its customer base, and disregarded the ephemeral nature of customer loyalty to a company. By 2010 Blockbuster filed for bankruptcy and became yet another footnote in the annals of business history.

Interestingly, Kaplan (2012) coined the phrase *Netflixed* as a reference to organizations that are so intransigent in their current business models, and so steadfast in their view of the superiority of those models, that they

NEW DIRECTIONS FOR COMMUNITY COLLEGES, no. 168, Winter 2014 © 2014 Wiley Periodicals, Inc.
Published online in Wiley Online Library (wileyonlinelibrary.com) • DOI: 10.1002/cc.20116

ignore the changing environment around them, even to the point of their own demise. In the community college context, competition from for-profit colleges, the increased availability of technology and online education, the rapidly changing demands of students and employers, and the advancing calls for accountability and fiscal efficacy threaten not only the current nature of community college funding streams, but indeed institutional viability overall. This particular and impending crisis must be faced head-on, with bold reexaminations of existing business models and financial structures so that community colleges can continue to serve student and community needs, innovate, and compete in a rapidly changing, digital, global, and highly volatile environment.

Among the many challenges faced by community colleges is the notable and substantial shift from state and local funding to a growing reliance on tuition and fees, without significant and corresponding increases in student financial aid, which has become a regrettable trend (Katsinas & Palmer, 2005). At the same time, community colleges face intense and growing demand to increase student access, retention, outcomes, and completion rates while serving more students at a reduced cost. Public concern about rising tuition levels, student loan debt eclipsing $1 trillion dollars, poor job prospects, and low salary levels in jobs after graduation has called into question the value proposition of a community college education. Indeed some have suggested, particularly inside the Washington, DC, Beltway, that higher education generally is broken. In light of these and other related trials, a perpetuation of the community college's current business-as-usual model is clearly inadequate for the future.

This chapter briefly traces the history of community college funding leading to the present-day crisis and describes its impact on the open-access mission of the community college. Additionally, this chapter considers the implications of this predicament on the work and responsibilities of college leaders and, by extension, their boards of trustees and staff, as they attempt to balance the growing demands made upon their institutions with diminished public subsidies. This discussion is particularly relevant given the current undertaking of the reauthorization of the Federal Higher Education Act (HEA).

Community College Funding: A Retrospective View

Contemporary community colleges emerged in the 1960s at rates approaching one new institution per week in response to new opportunities and demands that could not be met by the existing public junior colleges established in the early 1900s. Their three-pronged mission of transfer education, vocational education, and community service was to be realized through a solid financial model that included revenues from federal support, state support, local property taxes, student tuition and fees, and other minor, miscellaneous income sources. The exact level of total funding accounted for by each of these revenue sources varied by state, reflecting the states' differing expectations and goals for community colleges. For example, some state legislatures believed that tuition should be zero or very close to zero. Others suggested that funding streams should be relatively equivalent across the principal sources of state aid, local taxes, and student tuition. Still other states concluded that local property taxes should not be part of the funding picture. Regardless of the particular financial design, it was obvious that no one, perfect, uniform financial model would emerge nationally given the political, philosophical, and demographic diversity of the states.

Furthermore, regardless of the model used, community college funding has historically been unpredictable and unstable due to the discretionary nature of state support and the vagaries of funding initiatives. Breneman and Nelson (1981) noted that there have been routine periods of instability in the level of public financial support for community colleges, reflecting the competing priorities for government budgets over time. A study of the National Council of State Directors for Community Colleges further noted that the funding mix for community colleges not only varies considerably by state, but increasingly so due to both fiscal and policy pressures (Friedel, 2010). Within states too, funding streams can differ across institutions in local property tax support due to factors such as differing property valuations, differing tax levy rates set by boards, or different perceptions that local residents might have about the extent to which they are willing to financially support the local college. Not surprisingly then, the community college's experience of fiscal crises is not particularly new; indeed, they are nearly commonplace, though the quantitative and economic nature of each crisis and the attendant public and political attitudes vary (Lombardi, 1973).

However, funding mechanisms and related allocations for the community college cannot be evaluated independently of the institution's mission and its responsibility to the local community. Nor can funding be viewed independently from established federal and state priorities. Indeed, various levels of government can, and often do, provide funding incentives and/or penalties that seek to advance the public's will as expressed through Congress and state legislatures. A recent example can be seen in the Trade Adjustment Assistance Community College and Career Training program (United States Department of Labor, 2011) launched by the Obama administration in 2009, as part of the American Recovery and Reinvestment Act (ARRA). The enabling legislation provided $2 billion dollars over four years to fund community colleges that pursued, expanded, and improved programming around healthcare, information technology, and advanced manufacturing.

As part of this funding support, President Obama provided the states with monies for programs that enabled unemployed and underemployed persons to obtain training and marketable credentials as a means of advancing the economy. Many community colleges responded to this initiative by offering new, expanded, and accelerated programs, hiring faculty, opening new facilities, and purchasing additional instructional equipment. In Michigan for example, the effort became part of what then-Governor Jennifer Granholm called the "No Worker Left Behind" (NWLB) initiative, which provided up to two years' worth of free tuition to any Michigan community college, university, or other approved training program. Consequently, Michigan community college enrollments climbed until their zenith in 2012, due to the expiration of NWLB. Unfortunately, without such incentives, and faced with a recovering economy, Michigan community college enrollments fell significantly. Indeed, the Michigan experience is being played out across the nation, prompting employee layoffs, tuition increases, facilities reductions, classroom management strategies, and the exploration of new student markets.

If we have learned anything during the 100-year-plus history of the junior and community college movement, it is that the discretionary nature of funding from federal and state sources, combined with the vagaries of new funding initiatives, let alone other requirements of accountability and performance, has not provided community colleges with stable and predictable revenue streams. This type of revenue unpredictability, by definition, makes it very difficult for college leaders, boards, and system administrators to have any level of long-term confidence in budget development.

The Community College Funding Crisis

The progenitors of the community college could not have imagined the changed reality of funding problems faced by today's institutions; otherwise they would have taken steps to fiscally sustain and preserve their health so that they would continue to exist as the envisioned comprehensive, open-door, low-cost, and high-quality option for so many, particularly for those for whom there is no other option. Democracy's College stands in peril; its promise and hope for the masses are at risk. Indeed community colleges, now feeling the full effects of an improving, post–Great Recession economy, combined with lopsided sources of revenue and increasing demands for efficacy, are forced to make difficult decisions to keep their financial house in order, not all of them in the best interest of the students they are charged with serving.

To be sure, no single factor is to blame for this situation, as this fiscal issue has been historical and pervasive, though clearly its impact is expanding. Rather, each of the following elements should be considered in succession: declines in enrollment and the resulting loss of tuition and fee revenue even when tuition and fee rates rise, reductions in state aid, unsustained incentives, unfunded mandates, and rising costs.

Decline in Enrollment.   Lipka (2014) reported in *The Chronicle of Higher Education* that enrollment projections in the past routinely forecasted greater enrollments from one year to the next, though this may no longer be the case. Kindergarten enrollments across the country, a portent of things to come, have declined: "For every 100 18-year-olds nationally, there are only 95 4-year-olds. The Northeast and Midwest show the sharpest drop-offs. In less than a third of states, mainly in the West, can you find as many younger children as older ones" (p. 13). The clear implication is that funding streams tied to enrollment may decline in many states, a trend that can be exacerbated by net negative state out-migrations, declining birth rates, the relocation of businesses, and low college-going rates of high school graduates.

Additionally, students enrolling in the community college today are markedly different from those who enrolled a decade ago, not only in terms of ethnicity or socioeconomic status, but also in their preparation for college. Nationally, 60–90% of incoming community college students each year need developmental education support in at least one academic area (Bailey & Cho, 2010). The persistence and academic performance of students in developmental education is weak at best. Entering students needing assistance in mathematics, reading, and writing have little hope of completing their developmental program of study and enrolling into college credit classes, let alone completing an associate's degree (Complete College America, 2012). Fewer qualified and continuing students translate to reduced tuition and fee revenues for the college, and for many students, the outcome will likely be a poor academic record and the consumption of limited Pell funding for developmental courses.

Reductions in State Aid.   In its 2013 *State Higher Education Finance* report, the State Higher Education Executive Officers (SHEEO) organization noted that "in 2008, the Nation suffered the worst recession since the Great Depression. From 2008 to 2011, enrollment grew by an additional 13.2 percent; but state and local support, even with the assistance of the federal economic stimulus funds, stagnated, declining modestly for the Nation as a whole, and falling dramatically in some states" (SHEEO, 2013, p. 48). The report also stated that "appropriations per ... [full-time equivalent student] were lower in 2012 (in constant dollars) than in any year since 1980" (p. 19). Clearly these data would be more stark, in terms of overall decline in institutional revenues, had it not been for stimulus funds made available through ARRA. So, to a large degree, the future may be bleaker than it currently appears. More particularly for community colleges, declining state support has very real implications. For example, Kelderman (2011) found that in Iowa, state aid has declined to less than a third of the total revenues for community colleges there, while student tuition now pays for more than half of the colleges' operating budgets. In South Carolina, state appropriations as a proportion of total revenue have fallen to 40% in recent years with some technical colleges receiving as little as 10% in support.

In addressing the decline in state support, as well as the significant implications of these reductions, the SHEEO (2013) report appropriately notes that tough decisions will have to be made as colleges struggle to find ways to reduce student attrition, the cost of instruction, and time to a degree while improving instruction and increasing the numbers of students who graduate. Care will need to be taken to avoid quick, counterproductive decisions. As the SHEEO report notes:

> Avoiding bad judgments can be difficult when facing tough choices. Institutions may cut too many quality corners or compete with each other to raise revenue from "new" sources (such as out-of-state or international students) rather than make difficult decisions about priorities or the extra effort to create and effectively implement innovative practices. Policy makers may overestimate how many students can be well-educated within existing resources or make unrealistic assumptions about the potential for technology and new delivery methods to rapidly become a panacea offsetting the long-term negative effects of budget cuts or tuition increases on access to higher education and the quality of our workforce. Or the better-off public may be lulled into thinking that the American economy can get by with limited opportunity and 20th century standards for educational attainment, so long as their own families are well-educated. (p. 42)

The very real potential that today's fiscal crisis will be met by such misguided actions indicates that public higher education is not aware that, for many institutions at least, a Netflix moment may be upon us.

Unsustained Fiscal Initiatives and Unfunded Mandates. Another contributor to the funding crisis is the limited consideration given to the possible, unintended consequences of unsustained (i.e., temporary) funding/stimulus initiatives. For example, ARRA was a phenomenal program designed to jump-start the economy and put Americans back to work. As the flood of displaced and underemployed workers hit the community college classrooms, the colleges responded. They hired faculty and staff, provided wage increases, purchased needed equipment and software, repaired buildings, constructed new facilities, and expanded to meet the demand. Then, three years later the funding disappeared completely and community colleges were left to deal with the aftermath of an operational structure that was now overbuilt. Consequently, some colleges began to reduce support services to students, lay off employees, reduce contracts, and tighten budgets. In some cases, the effect of this abrupt conclusion of ARRA was staggering. For example, at Jackson College (MI), enrollment fell by over 33% in the succeeding three post-ARRA years, which was a reduction of nearly $8 million dollars on an overall operational budget of $48 million.

Additionally, federal and state reliance on competitive grants, focusing on government priorities as opposed to general base funding appropriations, has created a huge disparity among colleges, disadvantaging small, rural institutions, which constitute the majority of the nation's community colleges, but do not have the resources needed to employ grant writers. This gives a tremendous advantage to the larger, more affluent institutions. Relatedly, a base funding distribution of state aid, including both a core allocation and a portion distributed on the basis of enrollment, has now given way to varying levels of performance-based funding. The differing capacities of individual community colleges to meet performance expectations, given the diverse students these institutions serve, as well as the varying economic and geographic contexts in which they operate, could further disadvantage certain institutions, reducing their funding base and diminishing their capacity to serve students.

Other Contributors.   In addition to the aforementioned elements contributing to the funding crisis of community colleges, add the increasing number of unfunded mandates, as well as the hundreds of legally mandated federal and state reports that require time-consuming research, preparation, and reporting. Similarly, initiatives such as President Obama's (2014) desire for a 50% increase in the number of student completions by the year 2020 add to the challenges faced by community colleges without corresponding funding increases. Clearly this is a laudable goal, yet given the lean budgets of community colleges, how is such a goal reasonably accomplished without an infusion of resources?

Rising operational costs are also a fiscal reality facing community colleges. According to the American Association of Community Colleges (2014b), the average annual full-time tuition is currently $3,260 (in district). Boards and college administrations struggle mightily to keep these costs low so as to provide a pathway for every person to realize the American Dream. Yet, with the rising costs of running a college (i.e., utilities, materials, supplies, construction, salaries, healthcare, and benefits), the college is caught in the middle. Add to this situation the fact that there are increasing calls, from all quarters, for improved quality and accountability, including the use of scorecards, benchmarks, ratings, and other reporting methodologies (Field, 2014). The reality is that there is a cost to access, quality, and completion that must be acknowledged. Simply stating that graduation rates should be higher by a specific percentage, without an examination of the costs required to achieve that goal, is both simplistic and ill-conceived. If there is a public, social, and political will to advance the degree and skill achievement of Americans, then there is a cost to that level of achievement.

These and other trends are causing institutional leaders to grapple with new situations, scenarios, and rules that are unfamiliar to them. Not surprisingly then, colleges are making choices about how to keep things working in unfamiliar territory and experimenting with new approaches to fiscal sustainability, including caps on enrollment, differentiated tuition based on programs of study, capital campaigns, competency-based education, tuition discounting, international programming, guarantees, outsourcing adjunct faculty, new partnership structures, and a host of other items. It remains to be seen what the long-term impact of these new initiatives will be.

Implications for the Community College Mission

Given the funding challenges faced by community colleges, the idea of open access for all is jeopardized. Being "all things for all people" now seems unsustainable. Indeed the net effect of the current fiscal crisis is that many community colleges must now grapple with the painful truth of moving from a *comprehensive institution* that provides everyone with access to an affordable postsecondary education toward a *niche institution*, which, due to fiscal realities, may limit enrollments, offer only a few specialized programs (rather than a comprehensive curriculum), and offer some programs and services through external providers.

The movement away from comprehensiveness, for example, can be seen in the numerous California community colleges that have turned thousands of students away due to lack of resources for facilities, equipment, and faculty (Chen, 2014). Another example can be seen in the nation's rural community colleges, many of which are laying off faculty and staff, closing departments, or discontinuing other essential services, in part due to declining numbers of graduating seniors at area high schools. At Jackson College (MI), for example, enrollment in developmental programs has been limited to only those students who test at a sixth-grade level or higher, due to the high costs associated with advancing a student with lesser skills to college-ready proficiency. Other community colleges are facing similar choices.

All these factors notwithstanding, the three-part community college mission of transfer education, vocational education, and community service seems secure in its broadest form. However, stressed finances will have the impact of limiting the breadth and depth of programming in each of those mission components. As emphasized in the SHEEO (2013) report discussed earlier, institutional leaders will need to make choices about what programs and services to offer, as well as the level of quality that will be maintained for each. Given the potential for draconian reductions in the future, a timid approach to decision making is unwise. College leaders should declare early in the process that quality will be maintained at a high level for each operational practice, or the practice will be concluded. After all, student-consumers understand cuts but not poor quality, and should they experience low-quality programming, they will express dissatisfaction with their feet.

If community colleges are to sustain their relative mission, the biggest necessary change they will face is the adoption of a new financial and business model, such as a "niche design," that recognizes today's uncertain fiscal environment. Traditional sources and uses of funding are dynamic and changing for the long term. It is essential that institutional leaders begin planning for, and adapting to, these known and unknown changes immediately. An example of the need to deal with the unanticipated can be seen in Illinois, a state that has a large backlog of unpaid bills, potentially requiring colleges to fund a larger portion of their operational costs from other sources. Another example can be found in Statement 68 issued by the Governmental Accounting Standards Board (GASB, 2014). Outlining new accounting and financial reporting for pensions, this rule change has had the net effect of transferring the financial burden of state-provided pensions (for current and future college retirees) onto the community college's books, in the name of transparency. This change may potentially affect a bond rating company's assessment of a college's long-term liability, thereby limiting a college's ability to obtain long-term indebtedness at reasonable rates for construction or major projects. Both the fiscal developments in Illinois and the issuance of Statement 68 are examples of unpredictable events over which college leaders have no control. But in today's fiscal environment, leaders must be able to adapt to these events if their institutions are to remain fiscally viable.

In addition to being adaptable and flexible, the new business model must also provide some sense of institutional priorities while at the same time adopting safeguards that protect the organization from competitors, changing economic conditions, and potentially from organized labor. As an example of this priority setting, Jackson College Trustees have expressed a budget priority through a policy requiring that the college "pay itself first," setting aside 8% of the budget for instructional equipment, software, and facility maintenance off the top, before anything else is paid. Boards should also insist, by expression of policy, that the college maintain a fund balance of not less than three months' operating costs in anticipation of both opportunity and abrupt change. Additionally, policy should also provide for funding allocations for research and development, new initiatives, or experimentation to help sustain the college. Finally, the college's operations, and by extension, its budget, should also provide for new revenue streams from sources beyond tuition, fees, and federal and state revenues. Consideration should also be given to new costing strategies, partnerships, and business initiatives.

Leadership Implications and Strategy

Given the current view of success as a function of degree completion, all of higher education is progressively seen as broken, out of touch with cost escalation, and a poor return on investment. Accordingly, the likelihood of a return to financial levels of support during the late 20th century is minimal at best. Consequently, the community college president needed to shepherd today's community college must have a skill set that extends beyond time-honored abilities of statesmanship, budget setting, communication, and community leadership. Rather, the community college president must think in multiple dimensions, embrace calculated risks, innovate, create, explore, develop new relationships, develop new capital, network, think competitively, leverage resources, tolerate ambiguity, and document and communicate achievement. As an example, rather than going it alone, as in the past, colleges are collaborating in their pursuit of federal grants to improve their likelihood of success. Additionally, because the collection, use, and projection of meaningful and intentional data are essential in this new environment, investing in a solid institutional research department is vital. Analytics should help to inform the strategic plan, and by extension, the allocation of institutional resources toward targeted outcomes.

Other strategies for leadership consideration include remaking the community college into a "networked organization" that moves beyond mere collaborations, as in the past, to deep-seated relationships wherein resources and services are consolidated, shared, leveraged, and expanded to even larger markets and audiences. These networks must be built upon a deeper level of connectedness—in terms of communication, curriculum, purpose, and outcome—than the partnerships of the past. An example is the Community College/Career Collaboration project undertaken collaboratively by the American Association of Community Colleges, Goodwill Industries International, Inc., the Aspen Institute, Jobs for the Future, and three local community partnerships with Goodwill. This project is designed to "increase college and career success for low-income adults through documenting, promoting and replicating these models throughout the Goodwill and community college networks" (American Association of Community Colleges, 2014c, p. 1).

Agreements to preserve traditional boundaries and service districts make little sense when competition is aggressive, market-driven, commoditized, fungible, and highly competitive. Networks could provide a methodology for addressing competition from larger, differently motivated, and better funded organizations. These networks could include other institutions of higher education, state government, private industry, and even former competitors.

Likewise, thoughtful consideration of the "product" of the community college must be reevaluated so as to determine market relevance. For example, Carnegie units and grades are increasingly unimportant to employers. Grade inflation and continued uncertainty about what a particular letter grade means in terms of student knowledge and skills represent a challenge to the ongoing viability of our grading system. In its place, demonstrated mastery of specific technical skills, as well as communication, problem solving, cultural appreciation, and other essential skills, represents the new currency the business community seeks. Community colleges that do not concomitantly adapt their outputs to the environment will experience revenue challenges either through reduced enrollments, declining public support, or both.

Conclusion

This industry is in crisis: a crisis of mission, a crisis of funding, and a crisis of identity. The best strategy is to embrace the challenges of the present and future reality, provide leadership through it, communicate about it, take reasoned risks, and move forward despite the criticisms that will surely follow. Only then will community colleges have a reasonable chance of avoiding institutional stresses, unnecessary upheavals, and for some, the possibility of being Netflixed. As community college leaders guide their institutions through this crisis, they would do well to thoughtfully consider the work of 21st Century Commission of the American Association of Community Colleges. The initiative generated two reports: *Reclaiming the American Dream: Community Colleges and the Nation's Future* (American Association of Community Colleges, 2012), and the Commission's implementation report, *Empowering Community Colleges to Build the Nation's Future: An Implementation Guide* (American Association of Community Colleges, 2014a). Both reports provide meaningful discussion of examples and tools for trustees, presidents, faculty, and staff to use in the positioning of community colleges for the future. Indeed, these documents could also be used to stimulate campus conversations regarding the redesign of a niche community college for the long term, one that is fiscally and operationally sustainable in the pursuit of serving students.

References

American Association of Community Colleges. (2012, April). *Reclaiming the American dream: Community colleges and the nation's future. A report from the 21st-Century Commission on the Future of Community Colleges.* Retrieved from http://www.insidehighered.com/sites/default/server_files/files/21stCentReport.pdf

American Association of Community Colleges. (2014a). *Empowering community colleges to build the nation's future: An implementation guide.* Retrieved from http://www.aacc21stcenturycenter.org

American Association of Community Colleges. (2014b). *Fast facts from our fact sheet.* Retrieved from http://www.aacc.nche.edu/AboutCC/Pages/fastfactsfactsheet.aspx

American Association of Community Colleges. (2014c). *Goodwill Industries International, Inc.—Community college/career collaboration.* Retrieved from http://www.aacc.nche.edu/Resources/aaccprograms/cwed/Pages/goodwill.aspx

Bailey, T., & Cho, S.-W. (2010, November). *Developmental education in community colleges* (Issue Brief prepared for the White House Summit on Community Colleges). Retrieved from Community College Research Center website: http://ccrc.tc.columbia.edu/media/k2/attachments/developmental-education-community-colleges.pdf

Breneman, D. W., & Nelson, S. C. (1981). *Financing community colleges: An economic perspective.* Washington, DC: The Brookings Institution.

Chen, G. (2014). *Dire in California: More than 100,000 students turned away from community colleges and counting.* Retrieved from Community College Review website: http://www.communitycollegereview.com/articles/322

Complete College America. (2012). *Remediation: Higher education's bridge to nowhere.* Retrieved from http://knowledgecenter.completionbydesign.org/sites/default/files/387%20CAA%202012.pdf

Field, K. (2014, August 22). Obama plan to tie student aid to college ratings draws mixed reviews. *Chronicle of Higher Education.* Retrieved from http://chronicle.com/article/Obama-Proposes-Tying-Federal/141229/

Friedel, J. N. (2010). What does it all mean? In S. G. Katsinas & J. N. Friedel (Eds.), *Uncertain recovery: Access and funding issues in public higher education—Findings from the 2010 survey of the National Council of State Directors of Community Colleges* (pp. 7–11). Retrieved from University of Alabama Education Policy Center website: http://uaedpolicy.ua.edu/uploads/2/1/3/2/21326282/2010_directors_survey.pdf

Governmental Accounting Standards Board. (2014). *Summary—Statement No. 68*. Retrieved from http://www.gasb.org/jsp/GASB/Pronouncement_C/GASBSummaryPage&cid=1176160219492

Kaplan, S. (2012). *The business model innovation factory*. Hoboken, NJ: Wiley.

Katsinas, S. G., & Palmer, J. C. (Eds.). (2005). *Sustaining financial support for community colleges. New Directions for Community Colleges: No. 132*. San Francisco, CA: Jossey-Bass.

Kelderman, E. (2011, February 6). As state funds dry up, many community colleges rely more on tuition than on taxes to get by. *Chronicle of Higher Education*. Retrieved from http://chronicle.com/article/As-State-Funds-Dry-Up/126240/

Lipka, S. (2014, January 24). Demographic data let colleges peer into the future. *Chronicle of Higher Education*. Retrieved from http://chronicle.com/article/Demographic-Data-Let-Colleges/144101/

Lombardi, J. (1973). *Managing finances in community colleges*. San Francisco, CA: Jossey-Bass.

Obama, B. (2014). *Education: Knowledge and skills for the jobs of the future*. Retrieved from the White House website: http://www.whitehouse.gov/issues/education/higher-education

State Higher Education Executive Officers. (2013). *State higher education finance, FY 2012*. Boulder, CO: Author.

United States Department of Labor. (2011). *Trade adjustment assistance community college and career training grant program*. Retrieved from http://www.doleta.gov/taaccct/

DANIEL J. PHELAN *is the president and CEO of Jackson College, Jackson, Michigan.*

New Directions for Community Colleges • DOI: 10.1002/cc

2

The topic of budgeting and financial resources often strikes fear in the hearts of community college administrators and faculty, as they believe it is an arcane and complex art understood only by accountants and financial specialists. This chapter attempts to demystify the basic concepts involved in budgeting and addresses approaches to budgeting, cost allocation, and using budgets for planning and control.

Community College Budgeting and Financing Demystified

David S. Murphy, Stephen G. Katsinas

Contrary to what many fear, budgeting is neither an arcane nor a complex art. Rather it is a multipurpose management tool, and although accountants are involved in the preparation of a budget, the budget should always represent the administration's expectations and plans. After all, budgets are simply an aggregate forecast of expected financial events and transactions over a period of time.

At a time when revenue streams have been restricted and more attention is being focused on the cost of higher education, budgeting is a critical component of the planning and control process. Table 2.1 summarizes the revenue pressure that is being placed on community colleges (Kirshstein & Hurlburt, 2013). As shown in Table 2.1, total revenues per full-time equivalent (FTE) student declined by 2.1% from academic year 2000 to academic year 2010, with a notable increase in dependency on tuition rather than government support. The proportion of revenues per FTE student accounted for by government (federal, state, and local) appropriations and grants declined by 8.3% from 2000 to 2010 (in constant 2010 dollars). In contrast, tuition as a proportion of total revenue increased by almost the same amount (8.1%). Accurate and transparent budgeting is especially critical as state support remains unpredictable and institutions grow increasingly dependent on student tuition and fees.

A budget should result from and be tied directly to the documents that flow from the strategic planning process; the long-range strategic plan should support an institution's mission and vision statements as well as the

New Directions for Community Colleges, no. 168, Winter 2014 © 2014 Wiley Periodicals, Inc.
Published online in Wiley Online Library (wileyonlinelibrary.com) • DOI: 10.1002/cc.20117

Table 2.1   Average Public Community College Revenue per Full-Time
Equivalent Student, by Source, 2000 and 2010

	2000 Revenue (US$)	2010 Revenue (US$)	Percent Change	Percent of Total Revenue	
				2000	2010
Revenue source					
Net tuition	2,324	3,269	40.66	18.5	26.6
State and local appropriations	7,095	5,712	−19.49	56.6	46.6
Federal appropriations plus federal, state, and local grants and contracts	1,646	1,821	10.63	13.1	14.8
Other sources	1,252	1,310	4.63	10.0	10.7
Total operating revenue	12,317	12,112	−1.66	98.2	98.7
Private and affiliated gifts, grants, contracts, investment returns, and endowment income (PIE)	222	158	−28.83	1.8	1.3
Total operating revenue (with PIE)	12,539	12,270	−2.15	100.0	100.0

Note: Data are drawn from Kirshstein and Hurlburt (2013). PIE = "private and affiliated gifts, investment returns and endowment income" (Kirshstein & Hurlburt, 2013, p. 6). Data reflect constant 2010 dollars.

goals and objectives that it has set. Goldstein (2005) noted that a budget is ". . . a map guiding an institution on its journey in pursuit of its mission" (p. 1). Implementation of the long-range plan may require capital investments for physical facilities and equipment. Thus, the long-range plan serves as the basis for the development of a long-range capital budget. The capital budget, prepared with at least a five-year planning horizon, identifies both the projected costs of capital projects and the expected funding sources for those projects.

The long-range plan should also provide the basis for the development of a one-year operating plan. The operating plan should answer the question "What needs to be accomplished this year so that we make progress toward our long-range goals?" This plan provides the direction for the development of a one-year operating budget, which has two purposes. First, it formalizes the financial plan (both revenues and expenditures) for a fiscal year. Second, it provides a basis for performance measurement. Without a budget it is impossible, at the end of the fiscal or academic year, to answer the question "How well did we do?" Thus, a budget provides both a financial road map and a measuring stick against which performance can be gauged.

If budgets are not derived from plans, there is a risk that an institution will set goals and objectives during the planning cycle that it either has no intention of meeting or that it will not be capable of meeting. Although lofty goals and objectives may be formalized in long- and short-range plans, an institution's spending pattern, which details where the money actually goes, shows what it really values. As Guskin and Marcy (2003) observed, "Ultimately, an annual budget process of an institution represents the only concrete statement about alignment of an institution's practice with its vision of the future" (p. 19). Budgeting is not an ancillary process; it is a critical success factor for successful planning and control.

This chapter describes four key elements of institutional budgeting: the cycle of budgeting activities that connects revenues and expenditures to institutional goals; the challenges of allocating costs across institutional offices and academic units; the use of variance reports to analyze planned versus actual expenditures; and the effect that the fiscal requirements of accrediting bodies have on institutional budgeting. The chapter concludes with a brief discussion of factors that may impede the use of budgeting as an analytic tool for planning and fiscal control.

The Budgeting Cycle

The budgeting cycle, which includes a series of activities leading to the establishment of a college's operating budget, begins with the establishment of goals and objectives for the fiscal year, as well as assumptions that will guide the development of the budget. Goals and objectives should be derived from the operating plan, based on the long-term strategic plan. A budget is a forecast, and so assumptions are made about demand for services, prices, and sources and amounts of revenues and costs. These assumptions are key to the development of a viable budget; in fact a budget is only as good and accurate as the assumptions made prior to its development.

The budgeting cycle begins with the establishment of budgetary assumptions. These assumptions include projected retention, graduation, and attrition rates; the expected inflation rate; and, perhaps most important of all, the demographic and other assumptions used to develop an enrollment forecast. Historical enrollment trends can be used to model fall-to-spring and spring-to-fall enrollment patterns and to project future student headcount. Retention and graduation rates are then used to adjust projected fall and spring headcounts. Target headcounts for new freshmen, transfer students, and returning students are then computed as percentages of the adjusted headcounts. The enrollment forecast is the key to the budget because it drives the revenue budget. In addition, the revenue budget, which is based on the enrollment forecast, expected changes in tuition rates, and projected state and local tax support, provides the spending constraint. Most institutions are required to operate within a balanced budget and can't spend more than the revenues they generate. Thus, the revenue budget establishes the spending cap.

Unit budget requests provide guidance for determining how revenue will be allocated to line items or, in the case of responsibility center budgeting, to programs and units. A responsibility center is an organizational unit with an administrator who is responsible for actions taken, costs incurred, and results. The key issue facing administrators at this stage of the budgeting process is how to allocate scarce resources equitably while at the same time allocating funds in a way that will lead to long-term goal attainment.

Revenue is not collected evenly over an academic year. In fact, a majority of the revenue is collected at the beginning of each academic term. However, some states have moved or are moving to funding models where, in some cases, the majority of the revenues are collected near the end of the term. Thus, it is important that the budget for cash receipts forecasts both the amount and timing of cash receipts. Cash disbursements, however, occur more evenly over the academic year. By understanding the amount and timing of both cash receipts and cash disbursements, administrators can determine the potential need for short-term financing (i.e., short-term loans).

The revenue and expenditure budgets, along with their respective cash budgets, are then packaged into the operating budget. This cycle does not incorporate the budgeting of capital expenditures which, while usually done separately, will affect the operating budget to the extent that some of the funding for capital projects will be derived from operating funds.

Cost Allocation and Budgeting

One of the most difficult issues in both budgeting and internal financial reporting is the selection of the most appropriate budgeting and reporting units. This selection will determine the nature and extent of financial information that is provided to decision makers within the college. Unit budget requests, including requests for personnel, form the basis for the preparation of the expenditure budget and subsequently for financial reporting. The budgeting approach used, as discussed in Chapter 3 of this volume, will determine what budgeting and reporting units are used.

The determination of budgeting and reporting units also affects decisions concerning how and at what levels to allocate costs. In incremental or line-item budgeting, the line item becomes the salient reporting entity but may not be particularly useful for administrative decision making and control, other than to control expenditures. For example, a line item may be established in the budget for a specific department for copying costs. Reporting by responsibility centers under a responsibility center budgeting approach (discussed in Chapter 3 of this volume) provides more useful information for decision making and financial control, because each center is under the control of a specific administrator who has decision rights over resource use, and because the effects of decisions can be mapped to results. In addition, reporting by responsibility center provides a more accurate measure of the cost of performing a specific set of activities.

Responsibility centers, in addition to being classified as either cost centers (which incur costs but do not generate revenues) or self-supporting centers (which generate revenues that can be used to support their own activities as well as the activities of cost center), can also be classified as support-focused or student-centered units. Support-focused units are organizational units that provide services to other units within the college, but that do not provide direct services to students. A student-centered unit is an organizational unit that provides educational or ancillary services directly to students. Support-focused units are often also cost centers, whereas self-supporting units are most often student-centered units.

Examples of support units include those that are responsible for the operation and maintenance of the physical plant and those that are responsible for institutional support functions, including "general administrative services, central executive-level activities concerned with management and long range planning, legal and fiscal operations, space management, employee personnel and records, logistical services such as purchasing and printing, and public relations and development" ("Institutional support," n.d.). Academic departments and student services are examples of student-centered units. The cost allocation question is whether or not support-center costs should be allocated to student-centered units and, if so, how those costs should be distributed. The allocation of support-center costs to student-centered units provides the administrators of student-centered units with a more complete picture of the total cost of education. It also helps them realize that support-center services are not "free," and it provides an incentive to control the use of those services. In addition, the allocation of support-center costs makes it possible to compare the full cost of service provision with corresponding institutional objectives. All activities have associated costs, nothing is free, but not all activities add value or lead to institutional goal attainment. Administrators should identify and eliminate non-value-adding activities (and their associated costs) as well as activities that do not lead to the attainment of long-range strategic goals. Although the allocation of support-center costs to the student-centered units has some significant advantages, it also encumbers those administrators of the student-centered units with costs over which they have no control.

As noted above, the decision to allocate costs from support-focused units to self-supporting student-centered units raises the question of how to most appropriately allocate those costs. In general, the allocation of costs from one organizational unit to another should be based on a cause-and-effect relationship. That is, the activities of the unit to which costs are being allocated should, in a measureable way, cause the generation of costs in the unit from which costs are to be allocated. This implies that the activities and costs of each cost or support center must be analyzed to determine the most appropriate activity measure or cost driver to use for cost allocation.

Consider, for example, the allocation of physical plant costs to academic units. Physical plant costs may be related in some way to student credit hour (SCH) generation by academic units. However, physical plant costs may be more a function of square feet of building space assigned to or used by the various units. If the cause-and-effect relationship between physical plant costs and square feet used is stronger and more direct than the relationship between SCH generation and physical plant costs, square feet used should be adopted as the allocation base for physical plant costs. The use of cost drivers (the metric used to allocate costs) that do not have a clear cause-and-effect relationship with cost generation in the support unit can result in inaccurate and misleading cost assignment.

Other Budgeting Issues

Two other issues that are often encountered in budgeting for higher education involve budgeting for the effects of grants and contracts, and budgeting for intraentity transfers. Grants and contracts may be awarded for general expenditures, or they may be earmarked for a specific use. Funds received for general expenditure may be included in the revenue budget, and then the corresponding expenditures are made in accordance with administrative intent. When grants and contracts are received for a specific function or program, it is necessary to determine if the funds supplement or replace existing funding sources. If the funding document specifies that the funds must supplement but not replace existing funds, then no funds can be reallocated from the function or program that received the grant or contract. If, on the other hand, a grant or contract can be used to replace current funds, then some or all of the replaced funds can be reallocated during the budgeting process and used to support other activities.

Often one department (e.g., the college relations department) provides services to other organizational units within the institution. This presents an interesting costing and budgeting problem. Two common budgeting solutions for dealing with internal service departments, like college relations, are to provide the department with a budget and then to expect it to provide "free" services to other organizational units. The problem with this approach is that it does not require organizational units that request services to think about the cost of the services; after all, the service is perceived as being free. The other approach is to provide each organizational unit with budgeted funds for internal service activities like the development of a marketing brochure for a new program. The "cost" of the design of the brochure has been transferred from the college relations department to the requesting department. In theory, this results in more reasoned use of internal resources because administrators become aware of the cost of the service that they are requesting.

Transferring the cost of internal services from the department that provides the service to the requesting departments presents another interesting accounting problem, that of price setting. In short, should the price of the internal service be set so that it covers the direct, measurable costs of the service provided, or should it cover the full cost of the internal service. The full cost would include the direct costs and allocated indirect or overhead costs as well. Both methods have advantages and disadvantages and, because accounting is really a behavioral science, may lead to different consumption decisions.

Using Budgets for Planning and Control

As noted above, budgets are tools for both planning and control. The control component of budgeting is often overlooked. The simplest form of budgetary control is to compare the budget with actual performance and to identify both favorable and unfavorable deviations from the budget. Table 2.2 presents a simple, line-item-focused budget variance report. This report shows whether or not actual performance was congruent with the budget. However, it does not explain what caused deviations from expectations. To do that, further analysis is required.

Table 2.2   Budget Variance Report—Revenue and Expenditures per FTE Student

	Budget (US$)	Actual (US$)	Budget Variance (US$)	Percent Variance
Revenue				
Net tuition	3,000	2,800	(200)	−6.7
State and local appropriations	5,700	5,400	(300)	−5.3
Federal appropriations and FS&L grants	1,800	1,200	(600)	−33.3
Other sources	1,200	1,310	110	9.2
Operating revenue	11,700	10,710	(990)	−8.5
PIE	200	150	(50)	−25.0
Total operating revenue	11,900	10,860	(1,040)	−8.7
Expenditures				
Instruction	4,000	4,800	(800)	−20.0
Research	50	30	20	40.0
Student services	1,200	1,000	200	16.7
Public service	500	400	100	20.0
Academic support	1,000	850	150	15.0
Institutional support	1,800	1,925	(125)	−6.9
Operations and maintenance	1,200	1,300	(100)	−8.3
Net scholarships and fellowships	1,500	1,300	200	13.3
Education and general expenditures	11,250	11,605	(355)	−3.2
Other	600	500	100	16.7
Total operating expenditures	11,850	12,105	(255)	−2.2
Change in fund balance	50	(1,245)	(785)	−1,570.0

NEW DIRECTIONS FOR COMMUNITY COLLEGES • DOI: 10.1002/cc

Table 2.3   Budget and Actual Summary for Faculty Salaries

	Budget	Actual	Variance
Number of FTE faculty	200	192	8
Average salary cost per faculty member (US$)	62,000	65,300	(3,300)
Total faculty cost (US$)	12,400,000	12,537,600	(137,600)

Negative numbers in this variance report indicate unfavorable variances. Revenue variances are unfavorable (negative) when actual revenue is less than budgeted revenue. Expenditure variances are unfavorable (negative) when actual expenditures exceed budgeted expenditures. A budget variance report does not answer questions; it directs attention. For example an administrator might ask the question, "Why was instructional cost per FTE student $4,800 when we budgeted $4,000?" The next step in the administrative control process would be to formulate a hypothesis about what could have caused that variance, gather data, and test the hypothesis. This type of analysis helps administrators learn from both successes (favorable budget variances) and failures (unfavorable budget variances).

A more in-depth analysis can be performed by examining the factors used in budgeting and in generating actual costs. For example, assume that the budget assumptions forecast 200 FTE faculty members with an average cost (salary, taxes, and benefits) of $62,000. Assume also that an analysis of payroll at the end of the budget cycle indicates that the community college employed 192 FTE faculty members at a total cost of $12,537,600 or an average of $65,300 per FTE. This information is summarized in Table 2.3.

As shown in Table 2.3, there was an unfavorable faculty salary variance of $137,600 because actual faculty salaries exceeded the budgeted faculty salaries by that amount. Although this total variance shows that the institution spent more than it had budgeted, the total variance is incapable of explaining what caused the variance. To understand that, it is necessary to unpack the total variance into its two components: a faculty salary rate variance (FRSV) and an FTE efficiency variance (FTEEV). A rate variance explains the effect of paying faculty members more (or less) than had been budgeted. The efficiency variance explains the effect of using more (or fewer) FTE faculty members than had been budgeted. The calculation of both is explained below.

Given that

> Budgeted total faculty cost = budgeted FTE faculty count
>   * budgeted average FTE salary

and

> Actual total faculty cost = actual FTE faculty count * actual average
>   FTE salary

we can compute the two additional variances by holding either faculty count or average salary constant and varying the other variable. The FRSV is computed as

FRSV = actual FTE faculty count * (budgeted average FTE salary − actual average FTE salary)

or, using the data from Table 2.3,

$$FSRV = 192 * (\$62{,}000 - \$65{,}300) = -\$633{,}600.$$

The negative variance is unfavorable and in this case indicates that the institution spent $633,600 more on faculty salaries because of the $3,300 increase in the actual average FTE salary over the budgeted amount.

The FTEEV is computed by holding the average FTE faculty salary constant at the budgeted amount and varying the FTE faculty headcount. This is computed as

FTEEV = budgeted average FTE salary * (budgeted FTE faculty count − actual FTE faculty count)

or, using the data from Table 2.3,

$$FTEEV = \$62{,}000 * (200 - 192) = \$496{,}000.$$

This variance is favorable because the institution used eight fewer faculty members than budgeted and consequently spent $496,000 less than budgeted. The variances are summarized as (a) FRSV ($633,600, unfavorable); (b) FTEEV ($496,000, favorable); and (c) total variance ($137,600, unfavorable).

The total variance computed here is the same as that shown in Table 2.3. However, this analysis helps better explain what caused the $137,600 unfavorable total variance. Paying faculty members more than budgeted costs the institution $633,600 more than budgeted. This was offset by reducing the number of FTE faculty members, an action that reduced actual expenditures, when compared to the budget, by $496,000, resulting in a total variance of $137,600. This analysis highlights the effects of tradeoffs that administrators often have to make. The same type of analysis can be performed on any budgeted item when data on budgeted and actual amounts are available along with data on cost drivers (i.e., the activities that cause costs to be incurred).

Requirements of Government and Accrediting Bodies

Budgeting is a key component, although not the only one, in financial control. Governments (both federal and states) hold public institutions

NEW DIRECTIONS FOR COMMUNITY COLLEGES • DOI: 10.1002/cc

accountable for the use of allocated funds. For example, institutions that receive federal funds are subject to specific reporting requirements and may even be subject to federal audits. In addition, accrediting bodies require that colleges and universities comply with standards for financial management. For example, section 3.10 of the *Principles of Accreditation* established by the Southern Association of Colleges and Schools Commission on Colleges (SACSCOC, 2012) identifies standards for financial management:

> 3.10.1. The institution's recent financial history demonstrates financial stability. (Financial stability)
>
> 3.10.2. The institution audits financial aid programs as required by federal and state regulations. (Financial aid audits)
>
> 3.10.3. The institution exercises appropriate control over all its financial resources. (Control of finances)
>
> 3.10.4. The institution maintains financial control over externally funded or sponsored research and programs. (Control of sponsored research/external funds). (p. 32)

SACSCOC Standard 3.10.3 requires that colleges and universities exercise appropriate control of all financial resources. Planning for the expenditure of financial resources through the budgeting cycle is part of this process. So too is the preparation, analysis, and use of budget variance reports. The preparation of a budget is a wasted administrative exercise if the budget is not subsequently used to monitor performance and to make decisions about future actions.

Conclusion

Budgeting is a critical component in the administrative cycle which encompasses planning, the implementation of plans, monitoring results, and managing activities so that goals and objectives are met. A budget should be the financial control tool used to implement both short-range and long-range plans. However, budgeting fails to fulfill this role when there is a lack of congruence between institutional plans and the budget. This occurs when the strategic planning focus is not carried forward and used as the basis for developing budgetary goals, objectives, and assumptions.

The use of line-item or incremental budgeting also gets in the way of employing the budgeting process as a strategic management tool. When not sufficiently tied to the institution's planning process, line-item or incremental budgeting tends to perpetuate decisions that were made in the past and at the same time ignore current goals and objectives. The budgeting process itself may become a roadblock in the way of achieving strategic goals and objectives when this occurs.

Finally, although budgeting is usually viewed as a fairly technical and analytic process, it is subject to what Collins, Munter, and Finn (1987) have

New Directions for Community Colleges • DOI: 10.1002/cc

called "budgeting games," which are used by individuals to further their personal goals at the expense of institutional goal attainment. These "games" include, among others, the "all-or-nothing" strategy, in which advocates for a particular institutional function claim that if their budget requests are not fully funded, the function will have to be abandoned; the "friendship" ploy, in which individuals exploit personal friendships to secure the funding they want; or the "sacrificial lamb" approach, in which unneeded items are included in the budget with the understanding that they be "sacrificed" when requested or that they will provide a cushion if no "sacrifice" is ultimately required. All lead to the failure of budgeting as a strategic tool, and they often occur in tandem with information asymmetry—the possession of private information by an individual that is not shared with a decision maker and the knowledge of which would have been relevant to decision making. This kind of behavior often manifests itself in the turf battles and empire building that are often reflected budget requests. Administrators must not allow the technical and analytic intricacies of budgeting to blind them to the behavioral side of budgeting and the resulting problems that may emerge.

References

Collins, F., Munter, P., & Finn, D. (1987). The budgeting games people play. *The Accounting Review, 62*, 29–49.

Goldstein, L. (2005). *College & university budgeting: An introduction for faculty and academic administrators* (3rd ed.). Washington, DC: National Association of College and University Business Officers.

Guskin, A., & Marcy, M. (2003). Dealing with the future now: Principles for creating a vital campus in a climate of restricted resources. *Change, 35*(4), 10–21.

Institutional support. (n.d.). *Glossary.* Retrieved from Integrated Postsecondary Education Data System website: http://nces.ed.gov/ipeds/glossary/?charindex=I

Kirshstein, R. J., & Hurlburt, S. (2013). *Revenues: Where does the money come from?* Washington, DC: American Institutes for Research. Retrieved from http://www.deltacostproject.org/sites/default/files/products/Revenue_Trends_Production.pdf

Southern Association of Colleges and Schools Commission on Colleges (SACSCOC). (2012). *The principles of accreditation: Foundations for quality enhancement.* Decatur, GA: Author. Retrieved from http://www.sacscoc.org/pdf/2012PrinciplesOf Acreditation.pdf

DAVID S. MURPHY *is the chairperson of the Accounting and Economics Departments at Lynchburg College, Lynchburg, VA, and a senior fellow at the Education Policy Center of the University of Alabama, Tuscaloosa, AL.*

STEPHEN G. KATSINAS *is a professor in the Department of Educational Leadership, Policy, and Technology Studies, and director of the Education Policy Center at the University of Alabama, Tuscaloosa, AL.*

3

Several budgeting approaches have been initiated as alternatives to the traditional, incremental process. These include formula budgeting; zero-base budgeting; planning, programming, and budgeting systems; and responsibility center budgeting. Each is premised on assumptions about how organizations might best make resource allocation decisions. Though the incremental approach remains dominant, experience with the alternative approaches suggests key questions that can guide the work of community college budget developers.

Budgeting Approaches in Community Colleges

James C. Palmer

College or university budgets serve two purposes. The first is to account for and control the use of funds entrusted to the institution by students, private donors, and taxpayers. This is a relatively straightforward though time-consuming process, guided by generally accepted accounting principles and public statutes or regulations specifying when and how budgets should be reported. The second purpose is more complex and less understood: The budget reflects decisions about how unrestricted funds (those not tethered by law, board policy, or funder stipulations to a specific institutional office or program) are best allocated to help the institution achieve its mission. Thus, in addition to assuring fiscal accountability, budgets reflect implicit or explicit theories of how resources can be optimally used given the institution's stated purpose.

It is in the latter, theoretical light that the varying budgeting approaches employed at community colleges need to be understood. Each approach is structured on implicit assumptions about how the organization might best come to an understanding of how funding, appropriately allocated, promotes the community college's primary goals, including student learning, persistence, and degree or credential attainment, as well as other goals relating to workforce development and community service. *Incremental budgeting* is conservative in the traditional sense, relying on past experience for an understanding of how monies should be allocated. *Formula budgeting* turns

NEW DIRECTIONS FOR COMMUNITY COLLEGES, no. 168, Winter 2014 © 2014 Wiley Periodicals, Inc.
Published online in Wiley Online Library (wileyonlinelibrary.com) • DOI: 10.1002/cc.20118

to analysis, costing out the component parts of the programs and services needed by students and allocating resources accordingly. *Zero-based budgeting* starts from scratch, seeking insight by testing the assumption that programs and services offered in the past are still needed and, if so, to what extent. *Planning, programming, and budgeting systems* (PPBS) focus on the goals of college programs and services, resting resource allocation decisions on cost–benefit analyses that compare alternative ways of achieving those goals. Finally, *responsibility center budgeting* (RCB) takes a market-oriented approach, assuming that resource allocation decisions are best made by program or department heads acting in their own interests to maximize revenues for their respective college units.

Colleges rarely use any one of these approaches exclusively; hybrid models abound (Barr & McClellan, 2011). And however compelling the theoretical underpinnings of each might appear, none supersedes organizational politics and bargaining as drivers of budget development within colleges. But an understanding of the assumptions underlying each model suggests what it might contribute to the process of determining how scarce institutional resources should be allocated.

Incremental Budgeting

Where does budget development start? In the incremental or line-item approach, the previous year's budget allocations are the starting point. They are increased or decreased, usually, though not always, in a relatively uniform manner across line items (e.g., programs and units) depending on the revenues available in the new fiscal year (Barr & McClellan, 2011; Goldstein, 2005; Kretovics, 2011). This is the most common and enduring approach to collegiate budgeting (Barr & McClellan, 2011; Goldstein, 2005). An example can be seen in the incremental budgeting process employed by the Maricopa Community College District (2012), in which "Colleges/divisions receive changes to [the] prior year's base budget based on available resources for mandatory or requested expenditures" (p. 2). Maricopa's budget development guidelines specify that "additional or incremental resources" are based on "priority needs" that enable units to meet "externally driven mandatory expenses," such as rate increases in the state's retirement system; "internally driven mandatory expenditures," such as personnel "step increases, employee tuition waivers, [or] compensated absences"; and discretionary expenditures (subject to board approval), such as "employee salary adjustments" or "district-wide initiatives" (Maricopa Community College District, 2012, p. 5). The link between district plans and incremental allocations (emphasized in Chapter 2 of this volume) is clear.

The use of the previous year as a base for the next year underscores the premium incremental budgeting places on historical continuity. It also reflects the assumption that, barring outsized enrollment fluctuations or sudden and significantly large revenue declines, "it is likely that the way in which individuals and organizations spend their resources will vary only at the margin from one period to the next" (Goldstein, 2005, p. 164). Simplicity and equity are other advantages. As Barr and McClellan (2011) note,

> Advocates of incremental budgeting point out that the model provides equal treatment for units across the institution and reduces conflict or competition that can sometimes surround matters of budget. They [advocates] further observe that incremental budgeting is easy to implement and scalable across a variety of institutional models and situational contexts. (p. 71)

But will these traits serve community colleges well in an era marked by the funding uncertainties and fluctuations described by Phelan (Chapter 1 of this volume)? Although "incremental budget increases" may have seemed appropriate during the post–World War II growth years of the community college movement, when enrollment increases convinced policymakers that the "new institutions must be headed in the right direction" (Meier, 2008, p. 200), the practice of projecting past resource allocation decisions onto future budgets has been increasingly questioned in the wake of recurrent recessions and growing skepticism that public investments in higher education have yielded expected outcomes in terms of student persistence and degree completion. Writing at the cusp of the decades-long era of economic uncertainty that has characterized higher education funding since 1980, Chaffee (1981) warned against "budget drift"—the tendency of institutions to grow increasingly inefficient as budgets perpetuate past practices year after year, oblivious to changing educational needs that might require significant shifts in practices and, consequently, resource allocation. Contemporary observers of higher education budgeting echo these concerns, noting that the incremental approach may paper over the inefficiencies of poorly performing units when they receive the same marginal increases awarded to highly performing units (Barr & McClellan, 2011) and bypass an "examination of what is being accomplished through the base budget … [and] whether there are better uses for some of the resources" (Goldstein, 2005, p. 165).

Formula Budgeting

A more analytic approach to resource allocation decisions lies in the construction of formulas that tie budget decisions to actual program or institutional costs given projected demand (i.e., enrollment) (Goldstein, 2005). Efficiency in resource allocation is the intent; tying allocations to an understanding of actual costs will minimize the probability that college units or programs will be overfunded or underfunded given the work those programs or units are expected to do. The purported objectivity of the formula approach also lends the budgeting process an aura of fairness, "reducing political influence in budgeting" (Goldstein, 2005, p. 171).

Though formulas in the public sector are most often applied at the state level to allocate funding across institutions, they sometimes factor into budgeting processes at the institutional level (Barr & McClellan, 2011; Goldstein, 2005). Examples can be found at large community college districts, where formulas may be used to allocate monies across district institutions. For example, the Alamo Community College District (2013) employs a "workload-driven budgeting model" that "allows for the calculation of an allocation for instructional faculty staffing at each of the [district] colleges, based on past enrollment activity by discipline and additional projected enrollments" (p. 72). The model also calculates "appropriations for academic support, student services, institutional support, and operations and maintenance" (Alamo Community College District, 2013, p. 72). Similarly, the Los Angeles Community College District (2013) employs a "budget allocation mechanism" that factors in "minimum staffing and maintenance and operations … costs" (p. 165). Both illustrate attempts to distribute funds across organizational entities at least partially on the basis of cost. But the extent to which formula-driven mechanisms are used for internal resource allocation at community colleges nationwide remains unknown.

Despite the apparent objectivity of the formula approach, critics warn that formulas may simply give an analytic sheen to standard incremental budgeting. Speaking of state-level allocation formulas, Barr and McClellan (2011) note that allocation formulas are "retrospective in nature," reflecting "experiences that have already taken place" and easily rendered obsolete "in the face of suddenly changing environmental or marketing forces or when [institutions are] presented with emerging opportunities" for new educational programs (p. 70). This reflects Goldstein's (2005) observation that the retrospective nature of formulas "can discourage new programs or revisions to existing programs" (p. 171).

Zero-Base Budgeting

Alternatives to the incremental approach have occasionally found their way into community college budgeting. One approach, zero-base budgeting (ZBB), emerged in 1969 at Texas Instruments and was introduced into the government sphere by Governor Jimmy Carter in Georgia's budget for fiscal year 1973 (Pyhrr, 1977). Premised on the assumption that resources could be more efficiently allocated to the extent that unit heads periodically rethought their operations in a systematic manner, ZBB in its original format involved (a) identifying "decision units," which usually, though not always, correspond to programs or organizational units detailed in institutional budgets; (b) creating decision packages that analyze the costs and benefits of alternative approaches for carrying out the work of the unit; (c) rank-ordering the packages on the basis of those cost–benefit analyses; and (d) using the information gained in this process to prepare "detailed operating budgets" for the unit (Pyhrr, 1977, p. 2). Early advocates saw this as a way of turning the gaze of the organization away from the past and facilitating new thinking that incremental budgeting might inhibit. A 1979 publication of the American Management Association put it this way:

> The essence of zero-base budgeting is captured in its requirement to *search for alternative ways*. To those of you who feel threatened, we are not asking you to go *down to zero base*. Rather, we are asking you to start from scratch and imagine that your operation did not exist today. Then, as you reconstruct your operation *up from zero base*, ask yourself, would you do things the way they're done today? Or would you opt for an alternative? Would you perhaps consolidate, reorganize, centralize, combine, merge, decentralize, subcontract, automate, or do something entirely different? Or would you eliminate the effort all together? (Austin & Cheek, 1979, p. 2)

Although the number of higher education institutions that adopted ZBB during its heyday is not known (Birnbaum, 2000), occasional publications document instances of community college experimentation with this technique after the economic downturns in the 1970s and 1980s ended the era of consistent and predictable annual increases in public subsidies for higher education. In some cases, ZBB techniques were used to justify incremental funding beyond specified base levels. For example, an approach used in the late 1970s by a Pennsylvania community college required program budget managers to submit funding requests—based on an analysis of decision packages—to the appropriate dean at one of three funding levels: 78%, 85%, or 92% or more. Each dean then submitted a budget request for his or her area—at no more than 85% of current funding—to the College's Budget Development Committee, along with a list of priorities for additional funding beyond the 85% base (Alexander & Anderson, 1978). The Committee would then weigh the merits of these requests and develop the final budget. Requiring budget developers to justify increments beyond base levels set below current funding levels (e.g., 78% or 85%) typifies ZBB's emphasis on not only testing the assumption that more monies may be needed, but also the assumption that current funding cannot be pared down without diminishing program or institutional effectiveness.

In other cases, ZBB techniques were used to assess alternative strategies for achieving specific program goals. Luna (1978), for example, described how Rio Hondo College's Mexican American Cultural Institute employed ZBB analysis to assess the relative effectiveness of three alternatives for the Chicano Studies curriculum: the provision of associate's degrees in Mexican-American studies and in bilingual and bicultural education within the college's Department of Mexican Studies; an interdisciplinary approach in which faculty members across multiple departments would, under the direction of a full-time coordinator, offer courses leading to these associate's degrees; and the creation of a Mexican-American studies major in a new department created through the consolidation of three separate programs. Decision packages were created for each, allowing for a detailed comparison of the three alternatives in terms of personnel and facilities costs. The decision packages also specified expected benefits of each alternative, detailed how those benefits would be achieved, and speculated on the consequences of not selecting each alternative. Luna's document presents a rare look into the use of a budgeting approach (in this case ZBB) in analyzing alternative curricular approaches for a specific degree program.

A search of the ERIC database as well as the Dissertation and Theses database yields no documents, articles, or dissertations on ZBB at community colleges specifically after 1980. Birnbaum (2000) traces the demise of ZBB to numerous problems, including the substantial time and paperwork it requires, especially in the compilation and review of numerous decision packages; the tendency of political wrangling to outweigh dispassionate analysis in resource allocation decisions; the implied assumption that decision units are "discrete" entities that operate independently from one another; and the difficulty of assessing "intangible outcomes" (p. 59). These limitations were evident even during the 1970s. Foreshadowing Birnbaum's critique, a 1979 analysis of legislatively mandated ZBB outcomes for the Colorado community colleges concluded that ZBB had been a time-consuming effort that was based on flawed assumptions (similar to those discussed by Birnbaum) and led to diminished morale among college staff (Tollefson, 1979).

Yet ZBB in at least some form can still be seen in contemporary budgeting practices. The Collin County Community College District (CCCCD), for example, adapted a *zero-sum budgeting approach* in the early 2000s as a way of striking a balance between the continuity provided by incremental funding and the need to adapt district programs to a changing social and economic environment (Israel & Kihl, 2005). Under the zero-sum approach, "new expenditures are paid through cuts in existing programs or increases in revenue" (p. 83). Division managers with authority to "reallocate resources across budget lines and across departmental budgets in their division" develop proposed budgets that are "less than or equal to the previous year's budget" and may make "supplemental budget requests [that] allow for increased allocations for costs associated with" the district's strategic plan (Israel & Kihl, 2005, p. 83). Another example stems from Colorado Mountain College, which "opted for zero-based budgeting in 2009 at the recommendation of a quality improvement team" (Porter, 2012, para. 5). Under the plan, "administrators asked each campus's budget official to fill out a comprehensive spread sheet for all general fund expenditures. As part of the process, each expenditure had to be tied to one of the college's six strategic goals" (Kiley, 2011, para. 10). Rather than simply proposing increments to existing budgets, budget managers combed through expenditure items, determining which are still needed and which might need to be discontinued. The comprehensive ZBB process with its numerous decision packages seems not to have taken hold as an all-encompassing budgeting approach; its time-consuming nature makes it impractical given the small budgeting and administrative staffs at most community colleges. But the examples from CCCCD and Colorado Mountain College suggest that an important legacy of the ZBB movement was an enhanced awareness that budget development should consider, even in a less detailed manner, alternatives to what has been done in the past.

Planning, Programming, and Budgeting Systems

This focus on alternatives is also a key characteristic of the more complicated PPBS technique, which, like ZBB, emerged in the 1960s. The unit of analysis in PPBS is the program, which in the case of community colleges might include degree programs, community service programs, academic support services (such as libraries or student service programs), or any other programs with defined goals. Budgets emerge from detailed cost–benefit analyses of alternative approaches to achieving those goals, a process that requires a sustained commitment to quantitative analysis. As Goldstein (2005) explains, "goals and objectives and their desired degree of attainment must be quantified, along with the costs and benefits of the alternatives" (p. 167). In addition, "the projection of costs and program output over a number of years [is required] to provide a long-term view of the financial implications of those programs" (Goldstein, 2005, p. 167). PPBS represents the apotheosis of administrative attempts to scientifically achieve the greatest marginal benefit from each dollar expended.

Economic downturns requiring colleges to seek internal efficiencies, emerging computer technologies that facilitated data processing, and the enthusiastic advocacy of some state governments and higher education associations led many colleges to experiment with PPBS or home-grown variants in the 1970s (Birnbaum, 2000). But, like ZBB, this experimentation seems to have been short-lived, collapsing by 1980 under the weight of its time-consuming nature and proving to be simply incompatible with the sometimes amorphous nature of college outcomes as well as with the political realities of campus budgeting, which is driven less by analysis than by the competition between different college offices for scarce resources (Barr & McClellan, 2011; Birnbaum, 2000; Goldstein, 2005). Birnbaum concluded that "it was a glorious ideal but one doomed to failure" (p. 43).

Still, the legacy of PPBS can be seen in ongoing attempts to understand the link between outcomes and fiscal resources. This is most notably evident in recent analyses of the costs incurred by colleges in leading students to degree or certificate attainment, or to the obtainment of some other community college outcomes, such as transfer to a university. Examples can be seen in the work of Manning and Crosta (Chapter 4 of this volume) and Romano, Losinger, and Millard (2011). Both offer methodologies for costing out completions (i.e., transfer or attainment of a credential) in terms of the degree paths specified in college catalogs as well as the actual enrollment patterns of students as they progress through the curriculum. Though not the all-encompassing analyses envisioned by early PPBS proponents, these new cost studies may do much to help budget makers connect their resource allocation decisions to the goal of student persistence and attainment.

Responsibility Center Budgeting

The budgeting approaches discussed so far rest final decision-making authority on the college's top executives. Whether determined through the incremental, formula, or the ZBB and PPBS approaches, budget requests for departments and programs are sent up the line for approval. Many view this centralized control as a necessity during economic downturns, assuming that top-level administrators may be more willing to recommend cuts than those who lead the programs that will suffer those reductions. But others suggest that devolution of decision-making authority to program leaders with responsibility for generating revenues is a preferred approach, leading to more cost-efficient operations that are responsive to consumer demand (Stripling, 2010). This is the fundamental tenet of RCB. As Kretovics (2011) emphasizes in his discussion of the RCB approach,

> unlike planning within a centralized system where unit or departmental managers attempt to maximize their budget allocation from the central administration ..., in a decentralized model units must generate sufficient revenue to fund their priorities as there is no central pot of money. This requires unit level administrators to think more creatively and be more entrepreneurial. (p. 86)

Goldstein (2005) and Barr and McClellan (2011) note that under the entrepreneurial, decentralized RCM approach, organizational units are divided into *revenue centers* and *cost centers*. The former (referred to as "self-supporting centers" in Chapter 2 of this volume) generate revenues through tuition, the sales of services (such as contracted education), or other initiatives. The latter do not generate revenues but provide the support services needed by revenue centers to do their work; in the case of a college, cost centers may include "the library, human resources, and the budget office" (Goldstein, 2005, p. 172). Chargeback techniques are used to charge revenue units for the use of the services provided by cost centers. Ultimately, those who lead revenue centers are responsible for their units' fiscal performance and have the discretion to allocate resources as needed to meet revenue targets (Barr & McClellan, 2011). In some cases, those costs include a "tax" imposed on revenue centers that is redistributed to college units "that are unable to generate sufficient revenues to finance their operations" (Goldstein, 2005, p. 172). Responsibility centers can often carry over excess revenues into the next year. But when targets are not met, "the unit is responsible for addressing the shortfall through increased revenues or decreased expenses in the subsequent fiscal year" (Barr & McClellan, 2011, p. 76).

Despite great potential, the RCB budgeting approach has been employed primarily at universities rather than community colleges, reflecting the fact that university department heads have greater access to "alternative sources of revenue, such as contracts, grants, [and] alumni gifts ..." (Hall, Metsinger, & McGinnis, 2003, p. 3). Yet in the face of fiscal exigency, community colleges have occasionally experimented with approaches that approximate the RCB. For example, Tambrino (2001) notes that when the Iowa Valley Community College District was faced with imminent bankruptcy in the early 1990s, its new president turned to contribution margin budgeting (CMB) as a way of producing a "positive fund balance in one year" (p. 30). Under the CMB plan, each district unit "would receive credit for the income generated by it and be charged for all of its expenses, including applicable indirect expenses" (Tambrino, 2001, p. 32). In addition, the college provided "appropriate incentives for each unit to reduce costs and increase income" (Tambrino, 2001, p. 32). The intent was to produce efficiencies by making unit heads aware of the total costs of their respective operations in relation to the revenues their units generated. Prior to the implementation of CMB approach, the district had "operated under a full-cost and income accounting system that separated academic responsibility from budgetary authority" (Tambrino, 2001, p. 31). Although aware of the direct costs of their units (e.g., salaries and supplies), deans were not aware of indirect costs and had no incentives "for controlling unit expenditures or increasing unit income" (Tambrino, 2001, p. 31).

This reflects a key purported benefit of the decentralized approach inherent in RCB—making administrators aware of and responsible for the total cost of their operations, including those related to "facilities management issues, energy savings, space utilization, and other support services" (Kretovics, 2011, p. 87). Yet, as desirable as this may be, the capacity of RCB or its variants to affect revenue generation and efficiencies relies on much more, including—in addition to the availability of alternative revenues—the capacity of unit heads to alter hiring and other administrative and curricular arrangements. Entrepreneurial action may be constrained by ongoing obligations to tenured faculty members in a department, the stipulations of collective bargaining agreements, the strictures of the academic calendar and the credit system, or the requirements of specialized accrediting agencies (such as those stipulating a minimum number of full-time faculty members in nursing and other allied health programs). There may be many subunits within community colleges where the administrative discretion required by RCB is possible. These include continuing education programs, business and industry centers, or other revenue-generating operations outside of the college's academic core. But RCB's potential as a driver of efficiency in that core is doubtful.

NEW DIRECTIONS FOR COMMUNITY COLLEGES • DOI: 10.1002/cc

The Enduring Incremental Approach

The history of budgetary experimentation in higher education since the 1970s reflects an ongoing search for budget development processes that move beyond the incremental approach and drive institutional reappraisals of traditional practices. This search has been propelled by a sense that the ease and familiarity of incremental budgeting—the very features that have sustained it as an enduring administrative tool—exact a cost on the capacity of colleges to reallocate funds from one year to the next in ways that allow them to do more with less while at the same time responding to emerging educational needs and constituents. Goldstein (2005) puts it bluntly, arguing that the continued use of the incremental approach demonstrates that "for many institutions, the need for efficiency in some administrative areas outweighs the desire for effectiveness" (p. 165).

Yet the administrative efficiency of the incremental approach has much to commend it and need not come at the cost of institutional effectiveness. Looking to the past as a starting point in the budgeting process makes sense in the case of academic programs, which are changed only with a great deal of caution lest they become untethered from the curricula at universities to which students transfer, or lest they disrupt the continuity needed by students as they move through a curriculum over time. Conservatism in budgeting serves the intuition and students well.

Furthermore, this conservatism need not block consideration of changes that might be required in response to new developments in the college's environment. After all, the use of incremental budgeting does not necessarily thwart leadership efforts to encourage analyses of program costs (as emphasized in formula budgeting), initiate campus conversations that question long-held assumptions about how and why colleges do the things they do (a tenet of ZBB), analyze the link between fiscal resources and program outcomes (a legacy of PPBS), or increase awareness of program costs and of the ways those costs might be reduced (a key goal of RCB). As Wildavsky (1978) put it, "traditional budgeting does not demand analysis of policy, but neither does it inhibit it" (p. 508).

Still, disenchantment with budgeting approaches seems as prevalent today as it was during the economic upheavals of the 1970s that led to early experiments with ZBB and PPBS. Although 55.5% of the community college chief financial officers responding to a 2011 *Inside Higher Ed* survey indicated that "their current budget models" were very effective at helping their institutions manage "resources during good times," the proportions of respondents indicating the same level of satisfaction with their budgeting models were lower for "managing resources during difficult times" (40.5%), "helping us set/reassess institutional priorities" (32.4%), or "helping us develop business plans for new academic programs and services" (22.0%) (Green, Jaschik, & Lederman, 2011). Yet the real issue may not be the budgeting approach per se, but the ways those approaches are implemented.

New Directions for Community Colleges • DOI: 10.1002/cc

Further research will need to go beyond the budgeting formats themselves, examining how community college leaders employ the annual budget development process, in whatever form, to engage the campus in the work of allocating resources in ways that sustain the needed continuity of academic programming while at the same time responding to new demands.

References

Alamo Community College District. (2013). *FY 2013–2014 annual budget.* Retrieved from http://www.alamo.edu/uploadedFiles/District/Employees/Departments/Fiscal _Affairs/pdf/Fiscal-Year-2013-2014.pdf

Alexander, D. L., & Anderson, R. C. (1978). *Zero-base budgeting: An institutional experience.* Cumberland, MD: Allegany Community College. Retrieved from ERIC database. (ED154693)

Austin, L. A., & Cheek, L. M. (1979). *Zero-base budgeting: A decision package manual.* New York, NY: AMACOM.

Barr, M. J., & McClellan, G. S. (2011). *Budgets and financial management in higher education.* San Francisco, CA: Jossey-Bass.

Birnbaum, R. (2000). *Management fads in higher education: Where they come from, what they do, and why they fail.* San Francisco, CA: Jossey-Bass.

Chaffee, E. E. (1981). *The link between planning and budgeting* [NCHEMS Monograph 1]. Boulder, CO: National Center for Higher Education Management Systems. Retrieved from ERIC database. (ED310650)

Goldstein, L. (2005). *College & university budgeting: An introduction for faculty and academic administrators* (3rd ed.). Washington, DC: National Association of College and University Business Officers.

Green, K. C., Jaschik, S., & Lederman, D. (2011). *The 2011 Inside Higher Ed survey of college & university business officers.* Retrieved from https://www.insidehighered.com /download?file=insidehigheredcfosurveyfinal7-5-11.pdf

Hall, G., Metsinger, J., & McGinnis, P. (2003). *Decentralized budgeting in education: Model variations and practitioner perspectives.* Unpublished manuscript, Department of Educational Foundations, Leadership and Technology, Auburn University. Retrieved from ERIC database. (ED482686)

Israel, C. A., & Kihl, B. (2005). Using strategic planning to transform a budgeting process. In S. G. Katsinas & J. C. Palmer (Eds.), *New Directions for Community Colleges: No. 132. Sustaining financial support for community colleges* (pp. 77–86). San Francisco, CA: Jossey-Bass.

Kiley, K. (2011, July 12). Starting from zero. *Inside Higher Ed.* Retrieved from http://www .insidehighered.com/news/2011/07/12/colorado_mountain_college_adopts_zero _based_budgeting#sthash.KZDqx593.pzumgO1e.dpbs

Kretovics, M. A. (2011). *Business practices in higher education: A guide for today's administrators.* New York, NY: Routledge.

Los Angeles Community College District. (2013). *Final budget 2013-2014.* Retrieved from https://www.laccd.edu/Departments/CFO/budget/BudgetReports/FinalBudget /Documents/2013-14FinalBudget.pdf

Luna, P. R. (1978). *Zero-based budgeting: Application to Chicano Studies at a community college.* Whittier, CA: Rio Hondo College. Retrieved from ERIC database. (ED184624)

Maricopa Community College District. (2012). *Budget development handbook.* Retrieved from https://business.maricopa.edu/sites/default/files/fy15bgthandbook.pdf

Meier, K. M. (2008). *The community college mission: History and theory* (Unpublished doctoral dissertation). University of Arizona, Tucson.

Porter, M. V. (2012, April). Starting from scratch. *Business Officer Magazine*. Retrieved from http://www.nacubo.org/Business_Officer_Magazine/Magazine_Archives/April _2012/Starting_from_Scratch.html

Pyhrr, P. A. (1977). The zero-base approach to government budgeting. *Public Administration Review, 37*, 1–8.

Romano, R. M., Losinger, R., & Millard, T. (2011). Measuring the cost of a college degree: A case study of a SUNY community college. *Community College Review, 39*, 211–234.

Stripling, J. (2010, December 13). Your tub or mine. *Inside Higher Ed*. Retrieved from https://www.insidehighered.com/news/2010/12/13/budget

Tambrino, P. A. (2001). Contribution margin budgeting. *Community College Journal of Research and Practice, 25*, 29–36.

Tollefson, T. A. (1979). *FY 1978–79 zero-base budget review. The Colorado state system of community and junior colleges: A summary*. Denver: Colorado State Board for Community Colleges and Occupational Education. Retrieved from ERIC database. (ED174270)

Wildavsky, A. (1978). A budget for all seasons? Why the traditional budget lasts. *Public Administration Review, 38*, 501–509.

JAMES C. PALMER is a professor in the Department of Educational Administration and Foundations at Illinois State University, Normal, IL.

NEW DIRECTIONS FOR COMMUNITY COLLEGES • DOI: 10.1002/cc

4

Community colleges are under pressure to increase completion rates, prepare students for the workplace, and contain costs. Colleges need to know the financial implications of what are often perceived as routine decisions: course scheduling, program offerings, and the provision of support services. This chapter presents a methodology for estimating the cost of instructional programs for completers who follow the program's curriculum (program cost) and for students who follow a different trajectory, often not even completing a program (pathway cost). Together these measures provide important insights to guide decision makers.

Program Costs and Student Completion

Terri M. Manning, Peter M. Crosta

Introduction

Measuring cost has become critical for community colleges over the past five years. As economic conditions have deteriorated, record numbers of students have flocked to community colleges for retraining, whereas state support for higher education has decreased. Administrators readily know what it costs students to attend community colleges but may not necessarily know exactly what it costs colleges to educate students in different programs. In order to make better resource allocation decisions or improve production efficiency, it is important for administrators to have a framework for measuring and understanding program costs and related concepts (Belfield, Crosta, & Jenkins, 2014).

In this chapter, we discuss a way in which community colleges can estimate two important costs: costs for academic programs and costs for student pathways. As explained next, the two costs differ in that the program cost emphasizes instructional costs and assumes program completion, whereas the pathway cost does not. Both are important for understanding how community college students incur costs to the institution and to themselves and how changes in policy and practice may impact overall institutional cost and efficiency. We also present in this chapter an efficiency metric or cost per unit of output. The writers understand that there is a great variation across colleges and state systems in how colleges generate revenue and

New Directions for Community Colleges, no. 168, Winter 2014 © 2014 Wiley Periodicals, Inc.
Published online in Wiley Online Library (wileyonlinelibrary.com) • DOI: 10.1002/cc.20119

distribute funding by department. The model identified here would need to be adapted by each state to make it meaningful at the local college level.

However, before discussing cost in more detail, it is helpful to understand the revenue source of community colleges. Most community colleges are funded on the basis of varying formulas that take into account tuition, fees, and appropriations from state, regional, or county governing agencies derived from taxes and on the basis of student seat time in classes. In some states, local property taxes also generate revenue that is not associated with enrollments. Overall, community colleges are the lowest funded sector of education and receive a set dollar amount for tuition and a set dollar amount per FTE (full-time equivalent) student or credit hours from their respective states, sometimes without taking into account the actual cost variation among programs and courses (Century Foundation Task Force on Preventing Community Colleges from Becoming Separate and Unequal, 2013). Some states (such as North Carolina) have created tiered funding as an attempt to address the costs of second-year and/or technical programs with high equipment costs and low faculty-to-student ratios. Tiered funding in North Carolina began two years ago, after the data for this study were collected. Other states partially fund colleges on the basis of performance or completion of students in degree or certificate programs. This performance-based funding has already taken hold in many states and may become a reality for most community colleges in the near future. Ultimately, colleges generally will spend whatever revenue they raise, from whatever the source. This chapter is written from the perspective of a college under North Carolina's funding formula prior to the onset of tiered funding, but the general ideas and methods could be extended to other states.

Why Estimate Costs of Academic Programs

When community college administrators look at cost studies, they are typically observing economic impact studies that quantify the return on investment for a student who completes coursework or for the community that invests dollars in public education. Depending on the state, colleges may not typically break cost down to the unit record level (by discipline, by course) in order to calculate costs per student per course, which are the building blocks of all programs. But by calculating unit-record-level costs, colleges can understand the factors that affect costs, where changes can be made to increase efficiency, and where recruitment and retention efforts should be focused.

In many cases, managers of academic programs are able to see their own budgets but have no common metric to measure costs across courses and are unable to estimate the college's investment for a student to complete any given degree program. But all courses are not created equal. Some are "cash cows," those courses that generate large numbers of FTE and are inexpensive to deliver (e.g., speech, English, history), whereas others are very expensive to deliver and generate far fewer FTEs (e.g., engineering and nursing).

How to Estimate Program Costs

Program instructional costs (all costs incurred by an academic area or discipline in the delivery of courses) can be measured by anyone at the college who has access to financial and FTE reporting systems, but it is typically done by institutional research and financial services staff. Program costs can be estimated by utilizing the following: annual financial budget reports broken down by instructional department; regional, county, or other local funding sources; grants and contracts; FTE enrollment broken out by prefix and course; and credit hours calculated from FTE (e.g., 1 FTE = 32 credit hours in North Carolina). Cost can only be broken down as far as financial records can be obtained. For example, in some colleges, the behavioral sciences unit has one budget code that covers history, psychology, sociology, and so on. Cost can only be broken down to the department level, meaning that sociology costs and psychology costs cannot be differentiated from one another but will be the same. If the social sciences department has one budget code for each discipline, social sciences could be broken down to the discipline level. Budget codes assigned to departments are typically not assigned so that discipline areas can study themselves but rather for the ease of financial services staff to monitor budgets and conduct audits.

It should be noted that a great variation in calculating unit-level costs occurs across community colleges. In some colleges, equipment and technology are purchased and distributed through a central department, whereas at others those costs are allocated to the academic program or department. Once cost data are disaggregated by department and discipline, the data should be vetted by each academic area to verify or raise questions about data accuracy.

Table 4.1 provides an example of variations in instructional costs and reimbursement (revenue) levels for courses in various departments. The table shows some high-demand, low-cost departments (general education courses) and some technical program departments (higher cost courses). The cost column is generated from two key pieces of information: the FTE enrollment in the department and the total amount spent in that department's budget code on instruction. Cost is calculated on the basis of the instructional budget (revenue) for the program (including tuition and fees, FTE state reimbursement, county dollars, and grant funds) divided by the total credit hours generated (number of FTE times credit hours in an FTE).

In the 2008–2009 year, a student taking a three-credit-hour sociology course cost the college $115.38 (3 credit hours × $38.46), for which it was reimbursed (state appropriations) $302.52 (3 credit hours × $100.84). The college earned $187.14 more than it cost to educate the student. Keep in mind that if a student fails or withdraws from the sociology class and

Table 4.1   Cost per Credit Hour Versus State Reimbursement for
Sample Courses at Central Piedmont Community College, NC

Department/Program	2008–2009 Cost (US$)	2008–2009 Reimbursement (US$)	2009–2010 Cost (US$)	2009–2010 Reimbursement (US$)
General education departments				
Behavioral sciences (e.g., psychology)	38.46	100.84	44.02	99.77
Speech communications	58.02	100.84	54.64	99.77
English, reading, and humanities	41.59	100.84	42.53	99.77
Mathematics	37.28	100.84	39.60	99.77
Sciences (e.g., biology, chemistry)	42.66	100.84	44.74	99.77
Spanish	41.04	100.84	38.57	99.77
Art	63.82	100.84	56.70	99.77
Computer science	56.05	100.84	54.69	99.77
Technical program departments				
Cytotechnology	418.38	100.84	533.74	99.77
Mechanical engineering	208.18	100.84	206.16	99.77
Nursing	124.67	100.84	126.10	99.77
Dental hygiene	264.95	100.84	224.56	99.77
Nondestructive evaluation welding	119.54	100.84	113.34	99.77
Criminal justice	101.77	100.84	114.73	99.77
Culinary arts	109.02	100.84	87.26	99.77

Note: North Carolina reimbursements were not yet differentiated by program in 2008–2009 or 2009–2010.

retakes it the next term, the college will again be reimbursed $187.14 more than it cost to educate the sociology student. Technical courses do not result in a net positive dollar amount. If in the same year a student enrolled in a three-credit-hour cytotechnology course, it cost the college $1,255.14 (3 credit hours × $418.38) to educate the student, for which it was reimbursed $302.52. The college was reimbursed $952.62 fewer dollars than was spent educating the student. If this student fails or withdraws from the course and retakes it the next term, the college will lose another $952.62.

What Can Unit-Record-Level Cost Data Do for Your College?

Because departments have different costs associated with their courses, academic programs that combine these courses will have costs that also vary greatly. Degree programs consist of general education courses, entry-level courses in the major or related disciplines, and second-year courses in the major that lead to a degree. For example, the Health Information Technology program listed in Table 4.2 shows that students in this program take courses from 10 different disciplines that all have different cost amounts

NEW DIRECTIONS FOR COMMUNITY COLLEGES • DOI: 10.1002/cc

Table 4.2   Health Information Technology 2009–2010

Course	Credit Hours	Cost per Credit Hour (US$)	Total Cost (US$)	FTE Reimbursement (US$)
Required courses				
HIT 110	2	139.32	278.64	199.54
HIT 112	3	139.32	417.97	299.31
HIT 114	3	139.32	417.97	299.31
HIT 210	3	139.32	417.97	299.31
HIT 212	4	139.32	557.29	399.08
HIT 214	2	139.32	278.64	199.54
HIT 215	2	139.32	278.64	199.54
HIT 216	2	139.32	278.64	199.54
HIT 218	3	139.32	417.97	299.31
HIT 226	3	139.32	417.97	299.31
HIT 280	2	139.32	278.64	199.54
HIT 122	1	139.32	139.32	99.77
HIT 124	2	139.32	278.64	199.54
HIT 222	2	139.32	278.64	199.54
HIT 220	2	139.32	278.64	199.54
BIO 168	4	44.74	178.96	399.08
BIO 169	4	44.74	178.96	399.08
CIS 110	3	48.35	145.05	299.31
MED 121	3	79.88	239.63	299.31
MED 122	3	79.88	239.63	299.31
DBA 112	3	48.35	145.05	299.31
General education				
ENG 111	3	42.53	127.59	299.31
ENG 114	3	42.53	127.59	299.31
PSY 150	3	44.02	132.06	299.31
COM 110	3	54.64	163.92	299.31
HUM	3	42.53	127.59	299.31
MAT	3	39.6	118.80	299.31
Total	74		6940.423	7382.98
Profit or loss		Profit	442.56	

per credit hour generated. Although the Health Information Technology courses cost more to teach than was reimbursed from the state as FTE, the program made money for the college due to courses from 10 other discipline areas.

The three items that most influence the cost of programs are class size (total cost for a course divided by 30 enrolled students is higher than for 100 enrolled students), longevity/earnings of the faculty member, and high equipment needs for programs. Although colleges cannot always control for these issues, the following efforts can be made to decrease the numerator or increase the denominator and influence cost:

1. *Manage enrollment.* Make sure the correct number of sections is being offered to fill at 80% (or greater) of capacity. Efforts to increase

course completions and retention will also decrease costs and improve efficiencies (especially in high-cost programs where colleges spend more per credit hour than they receive in revenue).

2. *Consolidate programs.* Bring programs together that use similar equipment so that they can share microscopes, high-tech simulators, and technical equipment.
3. *Grow enrollment.* Bring in the marketing unit to help programs and courses grow their enrollment (potentially the quickest way to reduce cost).
4. *Take a look at the relevance of the curriculum.* Is it up to date? Is enrollment declining due to lack of employment opportunities in your community? It may be time to either reduce course offerings or develop an entirely new curriculum.

Colleges can also use cost data to raise funds within their communities. Students graduating from health programs such as nursing, dental hygiene, medical laboratory technology, and other high-demand majors are quickly hired by local hospitals and medical practices. Colleges can approach their community health organizations and ask for financial support in the form of scholarships or equipment to help subsidize or underwrite the costs of training these students. Organizations may be willing to participate, especially because corporate donations are tax deductible.

Why Estimate Costs of Student Pathways

Extending the method of determining program costs and combining it with longitudinal student data, one can compute costs of student pathways. This is important because the theoretical program costs discussed earlier often differ dramatically from the actual cost to the college as a student moves through her program of study once we take into account dropout and transfer. The program cost is one part of the pathway cost.

How to Estimate Pathway Costs

We introduce two concepts here that are related to the aforementioned program costs: the *pathway* and the *pathway cost.* A student pathway refers to the courses and services that a student consumes through his or her college career. This includes developmental education, traditional courses, online courses, student services, facilities, and administration. The pathway is fundamentally the student experience. The pathway cost refers to the costs incurred by the college for enabling the student to pursue an educational pathway. Pathway costs differ from program costs in three important ways. First, the pathway cost includes both instructional and noninstructional expenses. Second, the instructional side of the pathway cost will generally be different from the program cost as students move in and out of different programs of study. Third, the program cost assumes that a student completes his or her program; the pathway cost allows for attrition. Importantly, this means that, generally speaking, every student's pathway cost is unique.

As mentioned earlier, program costs emphasize the instructional cost associated with a program of study as determined by budget allocations to academic departments. They exclude the costs associated with administration, student support services, college operations, and facilities, which can comprise up to half or more of a college's overall budget. It is a challenge to determine how students incur such costs, however, since usage patterns will vary considerably and will be undocumented. For example, some students may make heavy use of the library, whereas others do not; a heavy library user can be thought of as incurring greater noninstructional costs than a light library user. However, advances in data collection could provide colleges with more granular information about actual usage of services and, therefore, enable institutions to make more accurate allocation decisions. Analysts can make any number of assumptions to estimate noninstructional costs associated with pathways, but they largely amount to a scaling factor applied to instructional costs. For example, using data from the Integrated Postsecondary Education Data System (IPEDS), one may estimate that noninstructional costs (e.g., cost of facilities, students services staff, administrative support, and libraries) may be one to three times the measured instructional costs.

Measuring pathway costs for completers and noncompleters is essential to understanding how different types of students incur costs and for calculating realistic average pathway costs for different programs or student groups. Programs with high attrition or early transfer rates will have average pathway costs that are considerably lower than the estimated program cost. Therefore, pathway costs that take into account the true student pathway will provide a much more realistic sense of the costs incurred by students to the institution.

The Efficiency Metric: Cost per Unit of Output

Taking into account completers and noncompleters is also essential to measure output-adjusted pathway costs. Adjusted pathway costs provide a way to compare program costs on a scale that corrects for student success in each program. In order to do this, however, it is necessary to have a measure of output. Although education is a multiple-output process, calculating adjusted pathway costs requires an output measurement that is quantifiable and can be distilled into a single number. In the past, we have used an output measure called associate-degree equivalents, which considers an associate in arts degree as one unit of output (Belfield et al., 2014). Other degrees and certificates are worth a proportional amount depending on the average number of credits graduates complete. For example, if a 64-credit associate degree is worth one unit of output, but the average AA holder graduates with 70 credits, a certificate where the average certificate holder earned 35 credits is worth 0.5 units of output. In the models detailed in Belfield et al. (2014), output was awarded only for completion or transfer but not for credits alone; that is, progress through credit accumulation is not considered output unless it results in completion or transfer.

Combining student pathway costs with an output measure enables the calculation of the adjusted pathway costs. More informative program costs result from the adjusted pathway cost. Consider the following example. The average pathway cost of 100 students who began college by taking developmental education courses is $15,000, whereas the average pathway cost of 100 students who began in college-level math and English is $30,000. Simply comparing pathway costs results in the conclusion that developmental education students are less expensive to educate than college-ready students. However, consider that the 100 developmental education students produce 10 units of output (developmental students complete credentials at a much lower rate than college-ready students) and the college-ready students produce 50 units of output. The adjusted pathway cost for all 100 developmental education students is $150,000 compared to the adjusted pathway cost of $60,000 for college-ready students: developmental education students are 2.5 times more costly to educate than college-ready students when considering both costs and outcomes. This exercise is not only useful for looking at different student starting levels but for comparing program-level costs. Which academic programs are the most efficient?

Consider the sample data shown in Table 4.3, taken from data at a North Carolina community college. The pathway costs are shown in Column 2, output in Column 3, and adjusted pathway costs (or cost per completion) in Column 4. Note that the college-ready pathway is more expensive than the developmental education (DE) pathway, but when adjusting for output, the cost per completion is much less expensive for students who start college ready. We also note, at this college, that students in allied health fields are more efficient than those in mechanics/repair programs even though the average pathway costs for these fields suggest that allied health programs are more expensive.

Changes in Adjusted Pathway Costs

Various community college reforms and interventions seek to reduce the adjusted pathway cost by either shrinking the cost of education or increasing the educational output. One question we might ask is how these interventions may impact expenditures and output. For example, a new student outreach program that identifies and provides support for vulnerable students may increase output for our developmental education starters but may also require additional resources. The intervention may, in theory, impact some students so that more developmental education starters complete the developmental education sequence and enter college-level coursework. What type of effect might this have on our cost model?

NEW DIRECTIONS FOR COMMUNITY COLLEGES • DOI: 10.1002/cc

Table 4.3   Pathway Costs, Output, and Costs per Completion

	Number of Students [1]	Pathway Cost [2] (US$)	Output [3]	Cost per Completion [=1*2/3] (US$)
All students in 2005–2006	3,810	13,970	477	111,310
Full time in first semester	1,530	19,580	271	110,660
Part time in first semester	2,280	10,220	206	112,930
Field:				
Allied health	111	30,560	24	142,050
Mechanics/repair	120	21,710	15	172,470
General liberal arts/science	1,460	17,250	222	113,300
Business/marketing	170	16,320	24	117,890
Initial placement:				
College ready	200	19,670	53	74,180
DE placement level 1	880	18,040	157	100,820
DE placement level 2	580	17,860	80	129,680
DE placement level 3	860	15,390	76	173,390

Notes: College credits only; not remedial education credits. Weights are based on the average duration to complete the award. Only data for curriculum (award-bearing) students are reported. Numbers rounded to nearest ten.

Source: Adapted from Belfield et al. (2014, p. 336).

One way to estimate the impact is to simulate the expected new reality using our existing data on student pathways. For the above example, consider that of those 100 developmental education starters, 50 complete the remedial sequence and 50 do not. Assume that an intervention is expected to increase the percentage of sequence completers by 20%, so that 60 complete the sequence and 40 do not. We can design a computer program (e.g., Stata, SAS, SPSS, or R) that allows us to simulate what the pathway's cost and output for this simulated student body might look like. That is, we can randomly replace developmental sequence noncompleters with sequence completers and calculate costs and output. Repeating this process 1000 times or so and averaging the results will provide an estimated average change in pathway costs and an average change in output. For example, the new pathway cost for our 100 developmental education starters (postintervention) may be $20,000, and the new output may rise to 15 units of output. The new adjusted pathway cost for the 100 students is $133,333, an improvement from the $150,000 shown earlier.

Conclusion

This chapter provides an introduction to various ways of thinking about program costs and efficiency in community colleges. First, we discuss a method for determining the instructional expenditures of complete academic programs and note the profit or loss to the college depending on the reimbursement rates for courses in particular disciplines. Understanding and comparing program costs using this method leads us to argue that colleges ought to think about managing enrollment, consolidating programs, growing enrollment, and redesigning curriculum as tools to manage costs. We then extend the program cost model to determine the costs for actual student pathways. We compare pathway costs for students in different academic programs or different college-readiness levels. We also adjust these pathways' costs for an output measure, which allows us to compare the production efficiency among programs.

It is important to highlight some limitations and risks of looking at program and pathway costs in this way. First, as noted earlier, it is not possible to accurately measure the noninstructional costs that are incurred by students. Better ways of measuring these are necessary in order to improve management of noninstructional spending. Second, the model is explicitly limited by the way in which a college performs accounting and budgeting. In our example, all courses in a department have the same cost per credit hour, but we know this is not true. Additional budget data would allow, for example, for lower level and introductory courses to be less expensive than for higher level and specialty courses within a discipline. Third, there are no clear guidelines for measuring output in the adjusted pathway cost models. We use associate-degree equivalents as an example, but output determinations should reflect the key outputs that the college is responsible for producing. There are many different ways to achieve this.

Suggestions for Practitioners

Measuring cost for courses, programs, and pathways is simply a way of estimating efficiency and effectiveness across programs at a given college. Although institutions of higher education may not like to see themselves as businesses with profit and loss statements, they cannot afford to lose money on every student in every program. They need to have a balance of cost across disciplines and courses. For colleges interested in studying the costs of courses and programs, the following suggestions are made.

1. Establish unit-record-level costs (by student by credit hour) for courses and programs and share it with midlevel instructional administrators (program, department, and division chairs/directors). By identifying and analyzing cost, people begin to understand it. Once it is understood, changes might be more easily made.
2. Be aware that faculty may not share an interest in reducing cost. They may also be concerned that many high-demand low-cost courses such as general education courses subsidize high-cost programs like nursing and engineering.
3. Use cost data as one indicator of the need for program revitalization, enrollment management planning, and marketing strategies.

The quickest way to reduce cost is to modestly grow enrollment in courses and programs (increases the divisor for cost), and to move students through programs while using proportionately less resources (sharing labs and lab equipment, for example).

4. Compare cost over multiple years to see if it improves.
5. Identify key student types and pathways where costs vary greatly, such as developmental students, undeclared majors, part-time students, and online students. Students may complete courses in any given semester, but their persistence to key milestones (e.g., completion of college-level math and English, accumulation of 15 or 30 credits) may be much lower than other student groups.

In this day of performance-based and completion-based funding, a pathway cost analysis can help a college understand where it is losing students and who is enrolling but not progressing. Once accepted, cost data can contribute to the increasingly important conversation around student success at any college

References

Belfield, C., Crosta, P., & Jenkins, D. (2014). Can community colleges afford to improve completion? Measuring the cost and efficiency consequences of reform. *Educational Evaluation and Policy Analysis, 36*, 327–345. doi:10.3102/0162373713517293

Century Foundation Task Force on Preventing Community Colleges from Becoming Separate and Unequal. (2013). *Bridging the higher education divide.* Retrieved from The Century Foundation website: http://tcf.org/assets/downloads/20130523 -Bridging_the_Higher_Education_Divide-REPORT-ONLY.pdf

TERRI M. MANNING *is the associate vice president of Institutional Research and founder of the Center for Applied Research at Central Piedmont Community College, Charlotte, NC.*

PETER M. CROSTA *is the director of research at 2U, Inc., headquartered in New York.*

5

A variety of policies and practices, including those developed by local boards and administrations, as well as those mandated by state and federal governments, affect budgets and finances at community colleges. Examples include tuition policies, fee structures, performance-based funding, and personnel policies. This chapter explores some of the reasons for policy changes and provides a framework for incorporating effectiveness into the community college mission, thereby avoiding unintended negative consequences for students or the fiscal viability of the institution.

The Implications of State Fiscal Policies for Community Colleges

Alicia C. Dowd, Linda Taing Shieh

Even before the Great Recession began in 2008, tax revolts and declining confidence in the public sector were eroding financial support for public colleges and universities. By early 2014, a survey of college presidents conducted by *Inside Higher Education* showed that despite improvements in the economy, higher education leaders disagreed with the statement that the economic downturn was "effectively over" (Lederman & Jaschik, 2014). This pessimism persisted despite the fact that 37 out of 48 states represented in an American Association of State Colleges and Universities (2013b) report experienced annual increases in state operating support in fiscal year (FY) 2014. In fact that uptick was part of a trend, building on an improved funding climate in FY 2013, when 30 states had increased public higher education appropriations, and in FY 2012 when 8 states saw increases. With fluctuations in the economy, fiscal issues still remain a chief concern for higher education leaders. More fundamentally, the character of community colleges seems to be changing and the damage from years of state disinvestment may be beyond repair. Although revenues lost during the recession may be slowly replenished, some fear that fiscal pressures have substantially changed the character of community college (Bohn, Reyes, & Johnson, 2013) and restructured higher education to the extent that public institutions are simply less "public" (Gonzáles, 2010).

NEW DIRECTIONS FOR COMMUNITY COLLEGES, no. 168, Winter 2014 © 2014 Wiley Periodicals, Inc.
Published online in Wiley Online Library (wileyonlinelibrary.com) • DOI: 10.1002/cc.20120

State dollars have been partially offset by shifting the burden to students through higher tuition and fees, but in most states colleges are making do with fewer resources (Zumeta, 2013). The situation varies by state, but a primary impact of fiscal belt-tightening in community colleges has been the number and variety of course offerings and the number of personnel available to assist students (Bohn et al., 2013). The weak economy has also increased legislative interest in policies that would compel colleges to use public funds more effectively to produce degree- and certificate-holding graduates.

This chapter discusses the impact of fiscal policies on community colleges and students. The following section elaborates on the policy context, discussing changes in tuition prices and enrollment demand as well as legislative interest in performance-based funding (PBF), which holds the potential to fundamentally restructure the conditions under which appropriations are provided to colleges. The impact of budget cuts on college personnel is then discussed.

Enrollment Pressures

If a for-profit firm were faced with fiscal pressures and uncertainty, we could analyze how well the CEO was responding to those pressures by looking at the "bottom line" of the firm's profits. However, college leaders are not corporate executives; they do not run profit-maximizing firms. In contrast to the CEOs of for-profit firms, who are said to be "profit-maximizing," college administrators are "resource-maximizing." Careers, programs, and institutions are built by responsibly managing greater resources, not by generating profits for shareholders (Ehrenberg, 2000).

The relationship between supply, demand, and price must also be modified when applying market perspectives to the public, nonprofit sector. Given that community college prices are subsidized, the enrollment demand tends to exceed the supply of courses. Community colleges do not necessarily suffer from a dramatic loss of "customers" when their prices rise. This is because the supply of courses is limited; there is a "fixed quantity subsidy" (DesJardins, 2003, p. 212) that pushes up demand for a community college education beyond the amount states wish to subsidize.

The Policy Context of Fiscal Pressures on Community Colleges

The divestment in public higher education following the economic crisis of 2008 translated into a greater decrease in per student resources at community colleges than in any other sector of higher education (Baum & Kurose, 2013, pp. 89–90). From 2005 to 2010, public associate's degree granting colleges experienced declining resources, resulting in a 5.3% decrease in average state subsidy per full-time equivalent (FTE) student (authors' calculations using IPEDS/Delta Cost Project data). Absent a diversified revenue portfolio, community colleges are especially dependent on and sensitive to fluctuations in state and local appropriations (Goldrick-Rab, 2010), which account for, on average, 41.1% of community college revenues. As teaching institutions serving local communities, community colleges are not as well positioned as other types of institutions to diversify their revenues.

To offset the loss of state subsidies, many colleges are attempting to expand nontraditional means of generating revenue. For example, greater emphasis is being placed on fundraising (Boyd, 2010). In FY 2013, over $200 million private fundraising dollars were added to community college revenue funds (Council for Aid to Education, 2014). Overall fundraising revenues increased across the board by 37.5% from FY09 to FY13, from close to $600,000 to nearly $900,000 per college at the median (Council for Higher Education Accreditation, 2014; Flahaven & Glover, 2010). However, philanthropic giving typically contributes only 1% of college revenues (Dowd & Shieh, 2013). Most community colleges cannot rely on private giving as a substantial source of funds.

Changes in Tuition and Enrollment

In times of fiscal uncertainty, attention to current trends in community college enrollment is appropriate for understanding the ways changes in tuition rates, course structuring, and the availability of postsecondary options in the for-profit sector may impact public two-year institutions. In this section, we explore how tuition costs, the provision of online courses at community college, and the for-profit sector is relevant to enrollment demand.

A Weak Relationship Between Tuition and Enrollment Changes. Tuition costs increased for community colleges in all states in the years following the economic crisis of 2008, with an average rate hike of 19% from 2009 to 2012 and 11 states imposing increases in the range of 20–35%. Compared with average tuition increases of 10% in 2006–2008, these statistics indicate that legislators in many economically distressed states were not able to observe typical constraints on annual tuition growth during the recession.

Given that tuition prices are subsidized, however, increases do not appear to drive dramatic changes in aggregate enrollment. Figure 5.1 illustrates the relationship between changes in community college tuition and fees and enrollment demand on a state-by-state basis in the years following the economic crisis (four states—California, Indiana, Louisiana, and Missouri—that had extreme changes that obscure the graphical display of the more moderate changes in the other states are omitted from this figure). From 2009 to 2012, 42 states raised tuition by 10% or more. In roughly half the states with tuition increases, enrollment also increased. The other half saw enrollment declines. Of the states omitted from the graph, California increased its relatively low tuition by 70% and reported a 12% enrollment decline. An estimated 585,000 students in California were turned away from 2008–2009 to 2012–2013 (California Community Colleges Chancellor's

NEW DIRECTIONS FOR COMMUNITY COLLEGES • DOI: 10.1002/cc

Figure 5.1.   Percent Change in Fall Enrollment Versus Percent Change in Average Tuition and Fees for U.S. Community Colleges From 2009 to 2012, by State

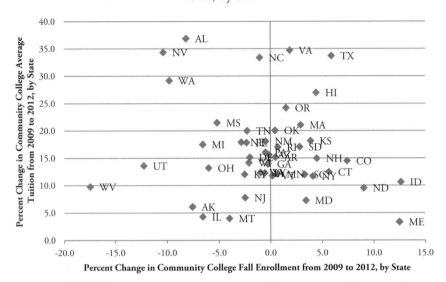

Source: Authors' calculation of NCES, Integrated Postsecondary Education Data System (IPEDS), fall 2012, institutional characteristics component. *Note*: Outliers CA, IN, LA, and MO were excluded from this figure.

Office, 2014). However, other states that increased tuition markedly did not experience enrollment declines.

The weak relationship between tuition increases and changes in enrollment indicates that community college enrollments, in the aggregate on a statewide basis, were fairly robust to the price increases of recent years. Factors other than tuition pricing, such as population growth, the supply of affordable options at other types of colleges, and the state economy, also have a strong influence on enrollment demand. It is not possible, therefore, to make a summary statement about the fiscal impact of tuition changes on community colleges, although tuition and fees contribute 16% of community college revenues on average (Dowd & Shieh, 2013). Although some colleges may lose students, and thereby tuition revenues, when tuition rates increase, others will not. In addition to the potential loss of students to other sectors of higher education, a college may lose revenue if it increases its tuition price and fees at a greater rate compared to other community colleges enrolling students from its same service area.

The fiscal impact on students is clearer. Those who cannot offset tuition increases with means-tested aid will immediately pay more now out of pocket or later in payments on interest for student loans. What an aggregate analysis of the relationship between tuition and enrollment does not address is whether low-income students were disproportionately lost from the entering student body and whether access became more or less equitable. Even if colleges don't lose enrollment (and therefore revenue), if more affluent students are available to take the place of low-income students, the disproportionate loss of low-income students undermines the community college mission of providing equal opportunity in higher education. This is of particular concern and emerges as a racial equity issue, as Latinos make greater use of community colleges as gateways to higher education.

Online Course Enrollment.   Community colleges have increasingly adopted online courses in their efforts to meet enrollment demand without overburdening on-campus classrooms. In 2008, nearly every two-year college (97%) offered online courses, compared to two thirds (66%) of all higher education institutions (Community College Research Center, 2013). A national survey of community colleges reported a 6.5% growth in distance education enrollments from fall 2011 to fall 2012 (Mullins, 2012). Although previous years saw larger rates of participation (22% in fall 2007 to 2008), this 6.5% increase juxtaposes with a 2.1% decrease in overall community college enrollment (fall 2011 to fall 2012), indicating that the online learning platform attracts students who may not be able to take classes on the physical campus.

Enrollment Demand Taken Up by the For-Profit Sector.   There is evidence of unmet demand, and redirected enrollments, in the growing number of Latinos in associate's degree granting and technical programs in the for-profit sector of higher education. The percentage of Latino students who initiated their studies at a for-profit college nearly tripled between 1995–1996 and 2003–2004, from 9% to 25% respectively (Soto, 2012). As a consequence of this shift in the postsecondary supply of education from the public to the for-profit sector, students face the risk of accruing unmanageable debt burdens. Among associate's degree graduates of any race or ethnicity, the majority (62%) who graduated from a public two-year college graduated with no debt (College Board, 2011). The fact that the majority of associate's degree holders were able to use a no-debt strategy for associate's degree completion is attributable to the relatively low costs of community colleges and to students' receipt of Pell grants, institutional aid, and state grants. During the recession (from 2008 to 2010), community colleges increased their expenditures on scholarships and student aid by 58% in order to meet the greater financial need of their students.

In contrast, graduates of the for-profit sector were the most likely to have accrued the highest levels of debt (compared to graduates from other sectors), and the vast majority of students (86%) took on debt (College Board, 2011).

Performance-Based Funding

The State Relations and Policy Analysis Team of the American Association of State Colleges and Universities (AASCU) 2013 report on state legislative agendas surmised that the "prevailing theme" for state higher education policy would be performance improvements "aimed at boosting measures of college affordability, productivity and student success" (AASCU, 2013a, p. 1). Interest in PBF, AASCU continued, is motivated by "the longstanding absence of additional state investment and new economic realities that beckon the need for better performance on measures of institutional productivity and student success" (p. 2).

> This has led states to turn attention to *how*—rather than *how much*—state funding is distributed to public colleges and universities....Institutions [are] incentivized to improve key *outcomes*, such as student retention and degree completion, and [give] less attention to boosting *inputs*, such as student enrollments. (AASCU, 2013a, p. 2)

Although its impact is uncertain, PBF is an important policy development because it changes the terms on which funding is provided by the states to colleges (Dougherty et al., 2014). Twenty-five states currently award and five have recently adopted legislation by which some proportion of higher education funds are distributed conditionally based on institutional indicators of student outcomes. These indicators include but are not limited to instructional expenses per credit hour of instructional delivery (Missouri), the number of degrees or certificates awarded per FTE (Tennessee), the ratio of administrative to academic costs (South Carolina), the number of credits students accumulate before transfer or graduating (Tennessee and Florida), and a time-to-degree measure known as a "graduation efficiency" index (Washington) (Jones & Snyder, 2012).

It is uncertain to what extent PBF has led to changes in institutional policies and practices, but the attention paid to low rates of student success by the Obama administration, national philanthropic foundations, and a variety of "college completion" initiatives has motivated changes at some institutions. For example, some colleges, such as the College of Southern Nevada, no longer allow students to register for classes three weeks after the start of classes because late registration is correlated with higher rates of student departure (Fain, 2014). Ending late registration has fiscal implications for colleges because most receive the majority of their annual appropriations based on FTE enrollment as measured at the time of an enrollment "census" date. When late registration deadlines precede census deadlines, a college will receive funding for all late registrants, even those who leave early in the academic term.

Given that early departure students do not require the resources of those who stay for an entire quarter or semester, colleges receive a funding premium for departing students. It is exactly this type of backward incentive that PBF is intended to dismantle. The fiscal impact of this type of policy change will be positive for colleges under certain conditions: (a) if course completion and term-to-term persistence rates increase among enrolled students and their enrollments "replace" the lost enrollments of those who would have registered late and (b) if appropriations are tied to performance indicators such as student persistence, credit accumulation, and degree completion. The fiscal impacts will be negative if late registrants are cut off from enrolling yet course completion rates do not improve.

Opponents of this type of institutional policy voice equity concerns that first-generation students who lack guidance on how to navigate college and low-income students who face more day-to-day uncertainty as to their ability to finance college will be most negatively impacted. However, college leaders can pursue equity in access at the same time that they adopt more efficient enrollment policies. For example, if registration policies are changed to restrict late registration and college data reveal that African American and Latino students register later in the term, on average, than other racial and ethnic groups, the college can become more proactive in reaching out to African American and Latino communities and schools with accurate information about matriculation requirements.

Fiscal Impacts on College Personnel

When state funding declines, something has to give. Figure 5.2 reveals the particularly close relationship between revenues and expenditures at community colleges. The top panel compares median per FTE student revenues across institutional types (categorized by Carnegie Sector), and the bottom panel compares median education and related (E&R) per FTE spending. Institutional expenditures decline in close relationship with decreases in revenues.

Community college's personnel costs typically consume 80–85% of state-provided operational funds. With revenue loss, the salaries of college faculty have declined, falling 2.5% in the most recent decade (from 2001–2002 to 2011–2012). In addition to decreases in base salaries, positions have been cut and benefits reduced. For example, a survey of California community college administrators conducted by the Public Policy Institute of California (PPIC) in 2012 revealed that 45% of California community colleges had implemented salary freezes and 32% had reduced benefits or kept them level. Among colleges yet to adopt such measures of fiscal belt-tightening, more than 70% of respondents indicated they were contemplating doing so. Employment levels fell nearly 8% from 2008 to 2011 (Bohn et al., 2013). Faculty unions appear to have played a role in insulating members from salary declines, as unionized faculty enjoyed higher salaries than their colleagues who were not unionized. However, the existence of unions at some colleges was not prevalent enough to fend off the cost-cutting trend toward part-time faculty (Thornton & Curtis, 2012).

Figure 5.2.   Total Median Revenue and Education and Related (E&R) Spending per FTE Student by Carnegie Sector (in 2010 Dollars), 2005 to 2010

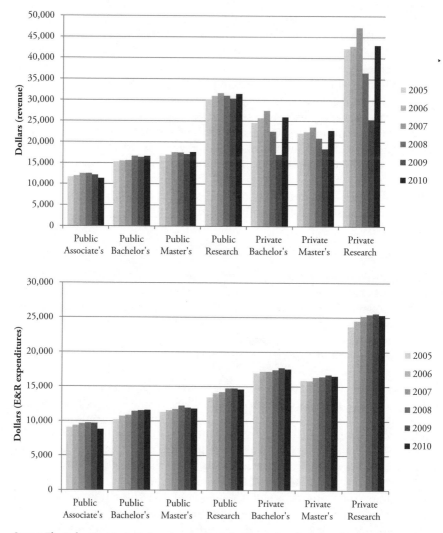

Source: The Delta Cost Project, American Institute for Research; calculations by the authors.

In great part, salary savings have been accomplished by replacing full-time faculty with part-time faculty, who tend to earn less and who are employed in community colleges in greater numbers than in any other sector (American Federation of Teachers, 2009; Eagan, 2007). Part-time faculty members now comprise 69.2% of instructors at two-year colleges (Council for Higher Education Accreditation, 2014). This surge in part-time faculty employment can be attributed to limits placed on hiring additional full-time faculty.

In addition to the decrease in full-time faculty, the number of staff employed in classified support roles is declining. The PPIC survey revealed that from 2008 to 2011, the percent change in the number of FTE employees in classified support roles decreased 15% in instructional support functions, 9% in positions classified as "other" student services, and 11% in ancillary services. These changes indicate that colleges were cutting back on services outside the core functions of instruction and administration. Given that the ratio of students to advisors already hovered around 1,000:1 in many colleges (Grubb & Gabriner, 2013), these personnel cuts indicate that fiscal pressures are creating a situation where students must be well equipped to navigate program and degree requirements on their own. State funding is not keeping pace with student demand for services (Katsinas, Tollefson, & Reamey, 2009).

The shift from a full-time to a part-time teaching force is generally viewed as a "neutral" policy in regard to student outcomes, but research indicates that this is not the case (Braxton et al., 2013). The fiscal impact of replacing full-time with part-time instructors may be positive in the short term but negative over the longer term, especially if appropriations are tied to student persistence and degree completion. The loss of instructors and the shift to part-time instructors translate into fewer class sections, larger class sizes, and less access to faculty advising. This coupled with the loss of student advisors signals trouble for first-generation students. College leaders can introduce equity safeguards as they assess fiscal impacts of policy changes by protecting advising programs and gateway courses that serve low-income and students of color from disproportionate cuts.

Incorporating Effectiveness Into the Community College Mission

As America's largest system of higher education, community colleges enroll nearly 40% of all U.S. undergraduates. Current economic, political, and social pressures on community colleges to effectively respond to state and national educational attainment goals have given rise to increasing legislative oversight on institutional operations and student academic achievement.

Democratizers of education, community colleges are tasked with the responsibility of serving populations with higher need, but provided fewer resources to do so. Per student public subsidies have declined. As (largely) open access institutions, the community college mission is diminished when public funding cuts restrict access. The fiscal impacts on colleges translate into impacts on students that deserve particular attention from an equity perspective. This is problematic for society as a whole, which relies on community colleges to provide a gateway to higher education, and for Latino students in particular who select community colleges over other types of institutions in large numbers, especially in the four states that enroll over one third of community college students in the nation: California, Florida, New York, and Texas. Pressures are mounting for improved effectiveness in producing graduates and greater efficiency in the use of public resources. To preserve democratic equality in access and equity in outcomes among different racial/ethnic and socioeconomic status groups, college leaders must articulate the importance of public support for community colleges at the same time they communicate their commitment to improved efficiency and effectiveness.

References

American Association of State Colleges and Universities (AASCU). (2013a, January). *Top 10 higher education state policy issues for 2013.* Washington, DC: Author. Retrieved from http://www.aascu.org/policy/publications/policy-matters/topten2013.pdf

American Association of State Colleges and Universities (AASCU). (2013b, July). *Fiscal and state policy issues affecting postsecondary education: State outlook.* Retrieved from http://www.aascu.org/policy/publications/aascu-special-reports/StateOutlookJuly 2013.pdf

American Federation of Teachers. (2009). *The American academic: The state of higher education workforce 1997–2007.* Washington, DC: Author.

Baum, S., & Kurose, C. (2013). Community colleges in context: Exploring financing of two- and four-year institutions. *Bridging the higher education divide: Strengthening community colleges and restoring the American Dream* (pp. 73–108). New York, NY: Century Foundation.

Bohn, S., Reyes, B., & Johnson, H. (2013). *The impact of budget cuts in California's community colleges.* Retrieved from http://www.ppic.org/content/pubs/report/R_313SBR.pdf

Boyd, J. S. (2010). *Essential personal attributes, skills and abilities needed by aspiring community college presidents* (Doctor of Education [EdD] dissertation). National-Louis University. Retrieved from http://digitalcommons.nl.edu/diss/27/

Braxton, J. M., Doyle, W. R., III, Hartley, H. V., III, Hirschy, A. S., Jones, W. A., & McLendon, M. K. (2013). *Rethinking college student retention.* San Francisco, CA: Wiley.

California Community Colleges Chancellor's Office. (2014). *Key facts about California community colleges.* Retrieved from http://californiacommunitycolleges.cccco .edu/PolicyInAction/KeyFacts.aspx

College Board (Producer). (2011). *Trends in student aid 2011: Trends in higher education series.* Retrieved from http://trends.collegeboard.org/sites/default/files/Student_Aid _2011.pdf

Community College Research Center. (2013). *What we know about online course outcomes.* Retrieved from http://ccrc.tc.columbia.edu/media/k2/attachments/what-we -know-about-online-course-outcomes.pdf

Council for Aid to Education. (2014). *Survey respondents by state: Voluntary support of Education (Report for FY 2013).* Retrieved from http://cae.org/images/uploads/pdf/VSE -2013-Survey-Respondents-by-State.pdf

Council for Higher Education Accreditation. (2014). An examination of the changing faculty: Ensuring institutional quality and achieving desired student learning outcomes. *CHEA Occasional Paper.* Washington, DC: Institute for Research and Study of Accreditation and Quality Assurance, Council for Higher Education Accreditation.

DesJardins, S. L. (2003). Understanding and using efficiency and equity criteria in the study of higher education policy. In J. C. Smart & W. G. Tierney (Eds.), *Higher education: Handbook of theory and research* (Vol. 17, pp. 173–219). New York, NY: Agathon Press.

Dougherty, K. J., Natow, R. S., Jones, S. M., Lahr, H., Pheatt, L., & Reddy, V. (2014). *The political origins of performance funding 2.0 in Indiana, Ohio, and Tennessee: Theoretical perspectives and comparisons with performance funding 1.0* (CCRC Working Paper No. 68). New York, NY: Community College Research Center, Teachers College, Columbia University.

Dowd, A. C., & Shieh, L. T. (2013). Community college financing: Equity, efficiency, and accountability. *The NEA 2013 Almanac of Higher Education* (pp. 37–65). Washington, DC: National Education Association.

Eagan, K. (2007). A national picture of part-time community college faculty: Changing trends in demographics and employment characteristics. In R. L. Wagoner (Ed.), *New Directions for Community Colleges: No. 140. The current landscape and changing perspectives of part-time faculty* (pp. 5–14). San Francisco, CA: Jossey-Bass.

Ehrenberg, R. G. (2000). *Tuition rising: Why colleges cost so much.* Cambridge, MA: Harvard University Press.

Fain, P. (2014). *Better late than never?* Retrieved from http://www.insidehighered.com/news/2014/03/05/college-southern-nevada-seeks-boost-retention-ending-late-registration

Flahaven, F., & Glover, T. (2010). *Community college foundations: An analysis of a survey conducted by the Council for Advancement and Support of Education.* Retrieved from https://www.case.org/Documents/WhitePapers/CCF_WhitePaper.pdf

Goldrick-Rab, S. (2010). Challenges and opportunities for improving community college student success. *Review of Educational Research, 80*(3), 437–469.

Gonzáles, J. (2010). *As government support shrinks, community colleges may start looking more like private institutions.* Retrieved from https://chronicle.com/article/Why-Community-Colleges-May/131636/

Grubb, W. N., & Gabriner, R. (2013). *Basic skills education in community colleges: Inside and outside of classrooms.* New York, NY: Routledge.

Jones, D., & Snyder, M. (2012). *Performance funding and strategic finance for higher education* [Powerpoint presentation]. Denver, CO: NCHEMS and HCM Strategists.

Katsinas, S. G., Tollefson, T. A., & Reamey, B. A. (2009). *Funding issues in U.S. community colleges.* Washington, DC: American Association of Community Colleges.

Lederman, D., & Jaschik, S. (2014). *Federal accountability and financial pressure: A survey of presidents.* Retrieved from http://www.insidehighered.com/news/survey/federal-accountability-and-financial-pressure-survey-presidents

Mullins, C. M. (2012). 2012 distance education survey results. *Trends in eLearning: Tracking the impact of eLearning at community colleges.* Washington, DC: Instructional Technology Council.

Soto, E. (2012). *Recruiting the growing minority: Latino enrollment practices in for-profit colleges and universities* [White Paper]. Retrieved from http://www.chci.org/doclib/20124131129386008-2012HigherEducationGraduateSummit-EnriqueSoto.pdf?trail=2012731184416

Thornton, S., & Curtis, J. W. (2012). *A very slow recovery: The annual report on the economic status of the profession 2011–12.* Retrieved from http://www.aaup2.org/newsroom/press/2012/12z/zreport.pdf

Zumeta, W. (2013). Higher education enters a new era. *The 2013 NEA Almanac of Higher Education* (pp. 27–35). Washington, DC: National Education Association.

ALICIA C. DOWD *is an associate professor in the Rossier School of Education at the University of Southern California and codirector of the USC Rossier Center for Urban Education (CUE).*

LINDA TAING SHIEH *is a doctoral student in the Rossier School's PhD program and a research assistant at CUE.*

6

This chapter explores the relationship between strategic planning and budgeting. It describes how community college leaders can use strategic and foundational plans (academic, facilities, technology, and financial) to drive budgets and resource allocations in support of institutional goals and objectives. Finally, it identifies challenges of doing so and the usefulness of budget decision packages as a way of determining the link between resource allocation decisions and the achievement of planning goals.

Linking Resource Decisions to Planning

Laura Saunders

An institution's budget reflects resource allocation decisions made at least partially on the basis of a strategic plan that articulates a vision for the future, a clear institutional mission, and defined values and educational goals. Strategic plans provide the framework within which these aspirations can be translated into operational plans (e.g., for programs and services) that are carried out through budget decisions. The effectiveness of the strategic plan can be measured and reported in terms of goal attainment as well as the actual financial costs of reaching the goals. Although this chapter is not about strategic planning per se, a brief review of the elements of a strategic plan sets the stage for a subsequent discussion about linking the plan to resource allocations (i.e., to budgets).

The Strategic Plan

A strong strategic plan is built upon an environmental scan, which may contain an analysis of the college's competitive position among education and training providers, and at least four more specific, or foundational, plans that are both shaped by and influence the strategic plan. The four key foundational plans are academic, facilities, technology, and financial plans. At some institutions, strategic plans may also be influenced by additional plans for enrollment management, advancement, student services, libraries, residence life, athletics, and other institutional functions (Hinton, 2012). All have budget implications.

New Directions for Community Colleges, no. 168, Winter 2014 © 2014 Wiley Periodicals, Inc.
Published online in Wiley Online Library (wileyonlinelibrary.com) • DOI: 10.1002/cc.20121

External influences are also brought to bear on a college's strategic planning efforts. For example, strategic plans at public institutions may have to align with system or state strategic plans and budgets that limit what an individual college can do or direct efforts to a statewide goal the college itself might not have identified as a priority. Krieger's (2011) discussion of how Kentucky approaches its budgeting and financial planning provides an illustrative example.

The bottom line is that, except in the rare instance when a new college is founded, strategic planning and budgeting will never occur in a vacuum; they will always be premised on what has occurred before and influenced by many internal and external stakeholders. The end result, though, is a sense of institutional direction. This is reflected, for example, in the strategic plan for Walla Walla Community College, a 2013 recipient of the Aspen Prize for Community College Excellence:

> The Walla Walla Community College strategic planning process is aligned and integrated with the College's core themes. The key elements framing the plan are vision, mission, the core themes, core goals or objectives, and core indicators. The Strategic Plan is an outcome reflection of current and historical data from College sources, economic and labor market analysis, demographic trends, an analysis of higher education in Washington state, and direct input from WWCC faculty, staff, and students, and members of the communities we serve. (Walla Walla Community College, 2014, p. 2)

Environmental Scans

Of particular importance in the strategic planning process is the environmental scan, which identifies emerging community needs as well as areas of declining emphasis. The environmental scan yields demographic, educational, and economic information about the service region, and enables institutions to build their strategic plan on the basis of a realistic portrait of the communities served. For example, the environmental scan prepared for McHenry County College (2013) by the Center for Governmental Studies at Northern Illinois University contains information about the district's geography; data on population demographics such as age, educational attainment, race/ethnicity, and income; and insights into area industries and occupations, including labor force participation. The scan looks not just at the current situation, but also includes projections that help the college assess what the needs and characteristics of its service district are likely to be in the years ahead.

The McHenry County College example is a highly sophisticated, multidimensional environmental scan that pulls data from a number of sources. Many institutions will lack the in-house skills or resources needed to hire external consultants to conduct this type of detailed scan. Nonetheless, it is critical for institutions to marshal the resources they can to gain a strong

New Directions for Community Colleges • DOI: 10.1002/cc

understanding about what is actually happening, and projected to happen, in their service areas. Few districts are immune from experiencing substantial changes over time. Assuming that districts are static will soon marginalize a college and reduce its capacity to serve the community.

Foundational Plans and Budget Implications

As noted earlier, colleges typically have four foundational plans that interact with the strategic plan. Sometimes one or more of these plans precede the strategic plan or have multiyear commitments that extend into the time frame for a new plan and must be incorporated in it. Sometimes the strategic plan itself sets a direction or broad goal that must be accommodated in subsequent foundational plans.

Academic Plans.   An academic plan begins with a review and analysis of the strengths and weaknesses of existing programs as well as potential new programs that either emerge from current curricula or represent totally new instructional areas. Academic plans also examine needed instructional innovations and the faculty development that will be needed to implement them. The environmental scan should provide key information about community needs and interests for academic programs, but information will also come from advisory committees, local business and industry leaders, and state and federal initiatives based on demand and supply in specific occupations. The academic plan developed by Cascadia Community College (2014) provides an example of a 10-year plan that has two specific foci: access and excellence. Within each, a number of objectives and action plans are listed, such as

- Enhancing interdisciplinary programs.
- Implementing the Bachelors of Applied Science in Sustainable Practices.
- Expanding learning communities and linked classes for new and continuing students.
- Exploring ways to further integrate STEM and Humanities programs.
- Developing new interdisciplinary Professional Technical programs/certificates in high demand occupations. (Cascadia Community College, 2014, p. 5)

This plan does not include specific timelines for accomplishing each action or more than a handful of quantitative target objectives. These might be spelled out in an accompanying operational plan that contains more detail and is suitable for annual revision.

The academic plan carries with it significant budget implications. Will new faculty, staff, facilities, or equipment be needed to sustain the quality of existing programs or to launch new ones? Are there start-up costs that will recede over time, or specialized accreditation that sets standards for program attributes such as student–faculty ratios or class sizes? Will the program require additional support staff to carry out functions such as managing admission processes for limited-admission programs or negotiating contracts with clinical and workplace sites? Is sustaining a weak program creating opportunity costs, that is, absorbing resources that could better be used for a different program? The academic plan clearly carries with it both direct and indirect budget implications.

Facilities Plans. Sometimes called a campus master plan, the facilities plan generally takes a long-term view because of the time needed to plan, secure funding, and build or extensively remodel major facilities. Keeping facilities consonant with the strategic plan and budget is crucially important, particularly because physical facilities are fixed. The El Paso Community College (2012) facilities plan is an exceptionally detailed document that includes not only a broad vision and guiding principles for the plan, but detailed analyses of space utilization, the condition of existing facilities, and projections for future enrollments. As the plan states on the cover page, "El Paso Community College's Annual Facilities Master Plan provides direction for facility acquisition, construction, remodeling, and maintenance." Because facilities planning typically covers a multiyear time horizon, creating an annual plan as detailed as this one may not be necessary.

Because of their long-term scope, facilities plans must often anticipate the unknown. For example, an academic building that does not have some built-in flexibility to accommodate unanticipated future needs (such as reserved space to accommodate future but as yet unknown developments in computer technology) may limit the capacity of an academic program to adapt to changing conditions. Flexibility in buildings comes with a price tag, and careful assessment of the costs versus the benefits of flexibility is important.

Additionally, as new approaches for supporting students emerge, facilities plans may highlight needs for new or remodeled spaces. For example, when many community colleges were first constructed in the 1970s and 1980s, providing spaces for students to "hang out" or to meet in small groups was rarely part of the facilities planning conversation. But today's emphasis on engaging students, employing group learning assignments, and increasing the scale and accessibility of support services (such as tutoring) has prompted colleges to rethink the purposes for which physical space on campus is committed and the degree to which those spaces are both functional and appealing. Colleges are also examining how the physical proximity of offices that provide services, as well as the traffic patterns to and from those offices, may encourage or dissuade students from using those services.

A decade ago, bringing together student services such as admissions, advising, registration, and financial aid in a single location was relatively novel. Today, numerous colleges have built "one-stops" to accomplish this, reducing the need for students to travel from one office to another, sometimes across campus, to access essential services. Colleges are committing space, even if in small amounts, to amenities such as "nap stations" and coffee shops within their libraries (Perez-Hernandez, 2014; Sinclair Community College, n.d.). Examples of facilities plans at community colleges, in addition to the El Paso Community College plan mentioned previously, include those developed by Oakton Community College (n.d.) and Austin Community College District (2007).

Technology Plans.   Technology planning is another cornerstone of the strategic plan. Looking into the future of technology can be very challenging because of the constant development of new products and upgrades to existing ones. Providing training that helps staff manage transitions to new systems is a real dollar cost as well as a cost in time and intellectual energy.

Technology is essential to colleges both in managing administrative functions and providing a platform and support services for instruction in virtually all subject areas. The goal of a technology plan should be to articulate a vision for the role of technology that can be used to develop budget requests and plans. Some colleges develop aspirational technology plans that start with a vision for technology and project future technology needs and costs. The information resources strategic plan at Bellevue College (WA) is an example (Beard, 2013). The plan posits three major components: the infrastructure layer, which focuses on "electronics and processing power that everything else relies on"; the information layer, which provides "evidence for decision making and assurance [that] the college is addressing its students' needs"; and the interaction layer, zeroing in on "web services, data integration and applications that empower staff, faculty and students with tools needed for success" (Beard, 2013, p. 3). The plan provides a framework for thinking about future technology needs in terms of hardware, applications, and projects. For example, the plan asserts:

> There is an incredible backlog of requests for services and tools....IR will utilize all available resources both internally and externally to prioritize and integrate those services ....Priorities will be based on the contribution of that service to student success and other components of the colleges' mission. (Beard, 2013, p. 6)

Though this conceptual model may seem somewhat ethereal and disconnected from money, it does provide a framework for thinking about future technology needs and the funds that will be required to meet them.

Financial Plans.   The financial plan is also a requisite for a strong strategic plan, providing estimates of revenue from sources such as tuition and fees, direct government support, investment earnings, local property taxes, partnerships, auxiliary enterprises, grants, philanthropic donations, and income from the sale of services or the rental of services. The institution also needs to plan for its short- and long-term indebtedness, and if it has the freedom to do so, to make strategic decisions about using funds from reserves, bond sales, or capital campaigns to fund facilities construction or other "big ticket" investments. If the college can set its own tuition rates and administer its own financial aid program, fiscal projections for both need to be made and included in the plan. If applicable, an institutional plan for tuition discounting is crucial in understanding the revenue actually available to meet the costs of operation. Colleges with large numbers of faculty and staff approaching retirement will also need to factor into their financial plans the costs of any college-funded retirement incentives or bonuses as well as the expected savings when new and presumably less-expensive faculty and staff are hired.

A three- to five-year financial plan, which is more general than a line-item annual budget, indicates how a program or service may grow and change over time. Programs and initiatives take time to mature, and it is imperative to consider their direct and indirect, short-term and longer-term resource costs. A multiyear financial plan must also incorporate a feedback loop that links evidence about progress in meeting a specific goal with decisions about continuing to support the initiative. As Murphy and Katsinas note in Chapter 2, budgets are for both planning and control. Though their example of control is based primarily on whether or not actual expenditures vary from budgeted expenditures, the concept of "control" can be extended to include determinations of whether or not expenditures, in the form of budget allocations, are supporting programs that are achieving desired goals.

Sometimes unexpected issues affect a financial plan. In 2013, for example, many colleges discovered that the Affordable Care Act's definition of *full-time faculty* would make many adjunct instructors eligible for healthcare insurance (see, e.g., Nelson, 2013). Colleges took a variety of approaches to addressing this unexpected challenge: reducing the number of courses an adjunct instructor could teach so as to keep the person below the eligibility threshold, creating new categories of adjunct instructors that made some (but not all) eligible for healthcare coverage, and reducing the number of course sections offered each semester as a way of reducing the need for adjunct instructors to teach multiple sections.

Linking Strategic Plans to Budgets

Institutional leaders frequently talk about linking plans to budgets, but actually doing so is challenging. In this section, a number of these challenges are discussed. All emphasize the fact that successful budgeting rests to a large degree on the leader's capacity to coalesce internal and external stakeholders around the goals articulated in the institution's strategic and foundational plans.

The Challenge of Priorities.   The link between a strategic plan and budget decisions involves analyzing the institution's goals in terms of resource requirements and setting priorities among the college goals. For instance, if a goal is improving student retention and increasing the graduation rates of students, the college may be faced with the task of determining which programs and services among the many suggested in the literature to implement. Making this determination will often require answers to several questions: What has the college attempted and what interventions are already in place? Do differences in achievement among student subgroups suggest that more intensive efforts need to be devoted to some subgroups to help them achieve at the desired level? Are the existing interventions effective and, if not, should they be dramatically revamped or even discontinued? Can the college afford to bring an effective intervention to scale; that is, to affect most if not all students? Should resource savings be returned to the college general fund or explicitly allocated to bring effective interventions to scale or launch new ones that have greater promise?

Setting priorities among the college's various goals is often the most difficult part of the strategic planning and budgeting process. The plan might include many goals, all of which are laudatory. But the budget can rarely support them all, and it is the budget that most concretely reflects the priorities. Depending on the campus culture, priority setting can be done annually in developing the budget, or over a longer period of time. It is impossible to overemphasize the importance of this step in the process. Without agreement about priorities, the budget decisions themselves will be mired in controversy.

The Challenge of Limited Flexibility.   Budgeting in community colleges takes place in an environment where resources are constrained and opportunities for growth can be limited. Often as much as 80% or more of the annual budget is already committed to existing staff, essential operations, and facilities overhead. New, undesignated funding is precious. Reallocation can be contentious. At the same time, "earmarked" or designated program funding may or may not relate to the goals in the strategic plan.

In addition, most community college budgeting is incremental in nature. Although zero-based budgeting had a brief period of popularity, reexamining budget allocations every year has proven to be difficult if not impossible in practice. Over time, however, incremental budget changes occurring at the margin can make significant changes in the direction of the college, particularly as it becomes clear that new campus initiatives and programs will be needed to reach agreed-upon goals. Savvy leaders who take the long view must manage the incremental budgeting process in ways that avoid the trap of blindly increasing funds for existing programs and services at the expense of other programs and services that will be needed if the college is to meet its goals in a changing environment.

The Challenge of Funding Formulas.   Governmental budget formulas may affect colleges differently; at some colleges, state funding may be 80–90% of the budget, and at others, state funding may be only 20–30% of the budget. Even within a state, reliance on government funds may vary across colleges. But regardless of the proportion of funds derived from these formulas, there is always the danger that they may not reflect institutional goals. For instance, they may reward seat time more than graduation. And although states have continually experimented with performance-based funding, the metrics used in those formulas may not accurately reflect the full range of student outcomes that a college hopes to achieve through its programs and services. These conditions make good planning and careful alignment of budgets with plans all the more important.

The Challenge of Leveraging Opportunities.   Though budgeting flexibility is limited, colleges often encounter opportunities to reallocate funds in support of programs and services aligned with the strategic and foundational plans. For example, when faculty vacancies occur, especially through long-planned retirements, institutions can move money to faculty positions in other programs or even to other positions entirely. (When student development faculty [counselors] retired at Oakton Community College in Illinois, for example, some faculty lines were replaced by full-time professional advisor positions.) Sometimes it is possible to convert several adjunct positions into one full-time, tenure-track position in a new area. Conversely, colleges can use unspent funds for a full-time faculty line in one program to subsidize several adjunct instructors in a new program for which the need for a full-time faculty member has yet to be determined.

The Challenge of Institutional Cultures.   Each campus has its own culture of budgeting and of implementing its plans. Where the culture treats these as separate processes that are only marginally linked, the likelihood of budgeting in support of plans will be weak at best. Moreover, broad plans that promise the moon can be invoked to support virtually any budget request. Thus, plans that include clear goals and measurable objectives, and institutional leaders who demand that budget allocations align with the plans are two critical components to ensure that institutional cultures will support rather than ignore or undermine plans. Two ways to build this culture are by engaging the campus in understanding the budgeting process and the budget's link to the plans, and requiring that budget requests identify how they support the plan.

The Challenge of Grants and Donations.   In Chapter 7, Drummer and Marshburn note the growing importance of philanthropy and foundations in providing revenue for community colleges. But the quest for additional revenues should be tied to the planning process. It is critical that all revenue sources—current and potential—be examined to determine whether they are aligned with the institution's plans. For example, a well-meaning donor might want to give funds to build a new swimming pool, but is the college prepared to commit physical space and annual operational funds to support an aquatic facility? Does having a pool comport with what the institution's environmental scan reveals about public and private sports facilities, including swimming pools, in the area? How does one gracefully decline a large contribution for a purpose that is outside the institution's

NEW DIRECTIONS FOR COMMUNITY COLLEGES • DOI: 10.1002/cc

plan, especially when the gift carries with it long-term financial obligations for the college?

Conversely, an institution's strategic and foundational plans may have goals that are unsupportable through existing revenues. Identifying grants, donors, contracts, partnerships, and business activities that can support the goal may be a productive effort. The costs of obtaining and administering these funds, including complying with what are sometimes burdensome reporting mandates, need to be included in considering whether to seek them. Intentionality in seeking support and the courage to say no are opposite and equally important sides of this challenge.

Translating Priorities Into Budget Decision Packages

In addition to strong planning and a leadership that recognizes and works against the challenges noted earlier, procedures must be in place to document and assess the link between resource allocation decisions and institutional goals. Although this is sometimes done through zero-based budgeting procedures that wipe the slate clean at the beginning of each fiscal year and construct the budget directly from goals articulated in institutional plans, the incremental budgeting that is more commonly used requires some sort of crosswalk between the budget and the organization's goals. Most budgets typically include line items organized under specific funds, programs, or departments. This accounting approach makes it difficult to understand or measure the resources flowing to a specific effort targeted to a strategic goal.

The creation of budget decision packages (BDPs) alongside college budgets is a useful way of addressing this problem. BDPs identify monies directed to specific initiatives regardless of which units, programs, or departments officially administer the funds. Perhaps this is best illustrated by using a typical institutional goal such as improving student success, which in this example might be defined as increasing the number of certificates and degrees awarded. After researching approaches to increasing completion for community college students, the college decides on a strategy it anticipates will foster completion: more mandated peer advising. A budget package can be proposed that includes training, stipends for student advisors, educational materials, and support for the administration of the program. The "official" budget might show that training falls within the professional development unit, stipends are in the student employee account, educational materials are in the library account, and administrative support is in the advising center budget. Looked at separately, these individual budgets obscure the resources that are targeted to improve the number of completions. But the budget package, which pulls the information together, provides a much clearer picture of the resources devoted to this goal and also enables evaluators to do a better job of assessing whether the funds spent are generating the desired results. In other words, is the end worth the cost?

Although developed initially as starting points for zero-based budgeting (Austin & Cheek, 1979), BDPs can complement incremental budgets by costing out specific planning initiatives and giving the college community a sense of what the resource allocation decisions reflected in the budget are intended to achieve. In addition, institutions may also require departments or programs to complete BDPs when requesting increased funding, helping to assure that funding increases are actually needed to meet organizational goals (see, e.g., Fayetteville Technical Community College, 2014). Finally, when colleges evaluate their plans, noting the extent to which planning goals have been successfully met, BDPs provide a basis for assessing the link between goal achievement and resource allocation.

Conclusion

Effective planning and budgeting are continuous and iterative processes. The mission, vision, and values articulated in the strategic plan may be revisited only occasionally, but the environmental scan should be regularly updated and reviewed. Foundational plans (the academic, facilities, technology, and financial plans) need periodic review as well. Rarely will a plan need to be redone from scratch unless it has been neglected or falls so far behind the institution's needs or current situation that it has become a historical, archaic document rather than a blueprint for guiding decisions. Strategic planning ought not to take place only occasionally, resulting in a document that gathers dust. At the same time, no institution can create a new strategic plan, which by definition is multiyear, on an annual basis. Rather, a balance between periodic and continuous planning, on the one hand, and annual or biennial budgeting, on the other hand, needs to be struck, with regular reporting on results in meeting strategic goals and objectives part of the institution's modus operandi. This can drive budgets that sustain movement toward desired goals.

References

Austin Community College District. (2007). *Facilities master plan*. Retrieved from http://www.austincc.edu/faoadmin/documents/SasakiFinalReport_2-28-07.pdf

Austin, L. A., & Cheek, L. M. (1979). *Zero-base budgeting: A decision package manual.* New York, NY: AMACOM.

Beard, R. (2013). *Bellevue College information resources strategic plan: Strategy versus reaction*. Retrieved from http://www.bellevuecollege.edu/ir/strategic-plan/

Cascadia Community College. (2014). *Ten year academic plan 2013–14 to 2023–24*. Retrieved from http://www.cascadia.edu/discover/governance/documents/ApprovedTen YearAcademic%20Plan%20Final.pdf

El Paso Community College. (2012). *El Paso Community College facilities master plan*. Retrieved from http://www.epcc.edu/sacs/planning/Documents/Facilities-Master -Plan-2012.pdf

Fayetteville Technical Community College. (2014). *Planning guide*. Retrieved from http://198.85.208.14/inst_effect/documents/FinalCopyof2013PlanningGuide.pdf

Hinton, K. E. (2012). *A practical guide to strategic planning in higher education*. Ann Arbor, MI: Society for College and University Planning.

Krieger, J. (2011). Community college budgeting and financial planning issues: A case study. In C. Rylee (Ed.), *Integrated resource and budget planning at colleges and universities* (pp. 32–41). Ann Arbor, MI: Society for College and University Planning.

McHenry County College. (2013). *Environmental scan*. Retrieved from http://www.mchenry.edu/excellence/MCC_Environmental_Scan_2013.pdf

Nelson, L. A. (2013, March 26). Counting adjuncts' hours. *Inside Higher Ed*. Retrieved from http://www.insidehighered.com/news/2013/03/26/groups-weigh-proposed-rules-affordable-care-act-and-adjunct-faculty#sthash.DLpyPmON.dpbs

Oakton Community College. (n.d.). *Facilities master plan*. Retrieved from https://www.oakton.edu/about/facilities_plan/

Perez-Hernandez, D. (2014, May 6). "Napping stations" at U. of Michigan library help students face exams. *Chronicle of Higher Education*. Retrieved from http://chronicle.com/blogs/wiredcampus/napping-stations-at-u-of-michigan-library-help-students-face-exams/52483

Sinclair Community College. (n.d.). *Sinclair dining services*. Retrieved from http://www.sinclair.edu/about/offices/aramark/

Walla Walla Community College. (2014). *Walla Walla Community College strategic plan*. Retrieved from http://www.wwcc.edu/CMS/fileadmin/PDF/Research_and_Planning/WWCC_Strategic_Plan_2014-2020.pdf

Laura Saunders retired after a career in community and four-year college administration, most recently as interim president of Bellevue College, Seattle, WA.

New Directions for Community Colleges • DOI: 10.1002/cc

7

As community colleges seek new revenue streams, philanthropic organizations, including college foundations and private funders, have already begun to influence both revenues and college programming. This chapter discusses the current role of philanthropy, especially private foundations such as the Lumina Foundation for Education and the Bill and Melinda Gates Foundation, to provide revenue and direction to community colleges. The chapter also explores untapped potentials and the role of local college foundations and alumni in contributing resources.

Philanthropy and Private Foundations: Expanding Revenue Sources

Carlee Drummer, Roxann Marshburn

In the face of the country's unprecedented economic challenges, private fundraising remains more important than ever to two-year institutions. Yet, although 44% of the nation's undergraduates attend community colleges, two-year institutions receive between 2% and 4% of all gifts "made to higher education" (Klingaman, 2012, p. 1). In 2007, the average benefit per full-time equivalent student from private donations, grants, investment returns, endowment income, and the like was $46,342 at private research institutions compared with $372 for community colleges (Century Foundation Task Force on Preventing Community Colleges from Becoming Separate and Unequal, 2013).

This gap may be understandable, given the differing missions of these two higher education sectors, yet the key social and economic roles played by community colleges suggest that these institutions can be of great interest to private donors and foundations and that efforts by the colleges to attract private monies can have a significant payoff. Ann Kaplan, who leads the Voluntary Support of Education survey conducted by the Council for Aid to Education, notes the vital role community colleges play with respect to the economic health and cultural vitality of the communities they serve. As a consequence, she emphasizes, "community colleges have an excellent case for charitable support—and should continue to assert that case for contributions" (Wilmington Trust, 2013, p. 3).

NEW DIRECTIONS FOR COMMUNITY COLLEGES, no. 168, Winter 2014 © 2014 Wiley Periodicals, Inc.
Published online in Wiley Online Library (wileyonlinelibrary.com) • DOI: 10.1002/cc.20122

77

Nonetheless, community colleges continue to struggle with bringing in the kind of donations enjoyed by four-year colleges and universities—a curious situation given the decline in state support for community colleges and the diminishing focus on higher education from state legislatures. Private funding, especially gifts earmarked for programs and equipment not covered through the annual operating budget, has become imperative to ensure academic excellence.

Although most community colleges in the United States emerged during the 1960s, development offices did not appear until the 1980s and even 1990s (Jones, 2010). Clearly, two-year institutions are late making the investments in fundraising that four-year colleges and universities started decades ago. The following explores the role of community college foundations in securing individual donations as well as community college efforts to work with and obtain funding from external philanthropic foundations.

Community College Foundations

Not surprisingly, more and more community colleges have established 501(c)(3) foundations to lead the push for private funding. Foundations bring a number of benefits to development efforts, including the chance to recruit and build a board of directors who focus on fundraising rather than college operations. However, given the scarcity of resources, most community college foundation offices remain woefully understaffed, with one or two people trying to accomplish the Herculean task of managing alumni relations, the annual fund, major gift solicitation, planned giving, scholarship programs, and special events. A recent survey conducted by the Council for the Advancement and Support of Education (Flahaven & Glover, 2010) confirms that community college foundations must rely on both staff and volunteers to achieve their missions.

The most productive foundation boards include individuals who share a deep commitment to the power of community college education and who are willing to initiate, cultivate, and strengthen community relationships and ultimately solicit donations. Typically a board member must satisfy two of the three Ts: time, talent, and treasure. For example, some board members who do not have discretionary income may bring other strengths to the table with respect to raising money. This reflects the familiar fundraising mantra of the three Gs: give, get, or get off.

In 2013, donations made by community college foundation board members to their own institutions accounted for 17.2% of all personal gifts to community colleges nationwide, exceeding the proportion (15%) of board members giving to four-year public institutions (Council for Aid to Education, 2013). This is a cause for optimism at community colleges. But foundation boards at two-year institutions cannot operate in a vacuum; community colleges must have strong presidential leadership that tirelessly supports fundraising efforts. Although current board members and the chief development officer most often assume responsibility for recruiting donors, "presidential presence in this process speaks volumes about the importance of the foundation to the college" (Teahen, Guy, & Byl, 2012, p. 13). In short, the president serves as the fundraising lynchpin, devoting a significant amount of time to the task and communicating the broad vision for the institution.

Fundraising Strategies.   Critical to any foundation's fundraising effort is the ability to listen—and match a donor's passion to a project. Diversified fundraising strategies—alumni giving, annual fund and major gift campaigns, planned giving, and special events—provide options for donors to become involved. In many cases, a prospective donor who attends a special event may be motivated to make a modest contribution to the annual fund, and several years later he or she may decide to establish an endowed scholarship fund or make a seven-figure commitment to a capital project. Many gifts to two-year institutions happen because of a meaningful encounter with a student who shares a compelling story about the life-changing experience of attending the community college. Regardless of the scenario, the key to raising money is cultivating a relationship and taking every opportunity to involve the individual in the life of the college.

Alumni Giving.   Although alumni relations programs in community colleges are beginning to gain traction, few community colleges have an alumni relations budget. Without robust revenue for staff, technology, and donor program development, community college alumni participation will continue to lag far behind alumni involvement at four-year colleges and universities. A Council for Aid to Education (2013) survey documents that only .08% of alumni identified by community colleges have actually made a gift, compared to 20.4% of the alumni at four-year institutions.

Nonetheless, given today's advanced technology, alumni relations offices can keep in touch with former students—with a minimum investment in resources—through electronic communication (e.g., e-newsletters, dedicated Facebook and LinkedIn sites, tweets, and e-mail blasts when big news breaks at the college). In addition, alumni relations offices, recognizing that the hectic lives of community college alumni often prevent them from attending special events, can focus outreach efforts on meaningful opportunities to give back, such as mentoring programs, visit days for prospective students, career fairs, and a lobby day at the state capital. (Keep in mind that alumni relations programs at four-year colleges and universities typically revolve around athletic events—an anomaly at most two-year institutions.) The bottom line: Alumni need to be engaged and inspired.

Klingaman (2012) makes a forceful case for developing a strong alumni association board that can support the fundraising work of the foundation. He notes that "the mission of the alumni association board will be to *give back* to the college. . . . Its purpose should be to develop an emerging leadership cadre from within the alumni" (p. 216). Alumni association boards should include representatives from the college's strongest affinity groups (e.g., athletes, nurses, student leaders, and thespians) and focus on projects that advance the goals of the strategic plan, such as student success. Alumni are advocates and should be the greatest ambassadors for the college; their active engagement enhances the college's reputation in the community. Thinking ahead, community colleges also need to remember that students are "alumni in residence" and engage them early on as well. Even alumni who transfer to a four-year college or university may come to recognize later in life that the community college indeed provided the best learning experience.

Annual Fund and Major Gift Campaigns.   The core of the collegiate fundraising model, the annual fund provides the opportunity for sustainable, repeatable gifts on a yearly basis. Annual giving campaigns can touch the entire community—alumni and nonalumni, businesses, corporations, employees, and board members—and boost awareness of the wonderful work being accomplished at the college. Development offices should set achievable annual giving goals that increase incrementally each year. Annual fund gifts are especially important from board members who should donate an amount that a peer would consider to be generous (Klingaman, 2012).

Cultivating individual donors heads the list for successful annual giving campaigns. Whether they are entrepreneurs, small business owners, retirees, or corporate magnates, they are people who value the community college mission of transforming lives and enhancing the local economy. Early in their careers, development professionals hear this advice: "Spend 100 percent of your time going for 100 percent of the gifts" (Jones, 2010, p. 17). Looking at the typical community college gift pyramid, 95% of donations come from 5% of the donors. That means development staff should be spending 95% of their time on 5% of the donors (Jones, 2010).

An often overlooked resource for the annual fund is the matching gift provided by corporations or individuals who have an interest in the institution and want to double or even triple the value of their donation. "65 percent of Fortune 500 companies offer matching gift programs" (Double the Donation, 2014, Matching Gift Statistics section, para. 1). Moreover, "mentioning matching gifts in fundraising appeals results in a 71% increase in the response rate and a 51% increase in the average donation amount" (Double the Donation, 2014, Matching Gift Statistics section, para. 7).

Major gift campaigns provide the opportunity to further cultivate individuals who consistently support the annual fund. However, with their limited staff, community college development offices face a daunting challenge to solicit and close major gifts. According to a survey conducted by fundraising consultants Bentz, Whaley, and Flessner, major gift officers in four-year institutions typically make "150 to 180 face-to-face visits" per year (Klingaman, 2012, p. 209). For a college employee working a five-day week with 10 annual holidays—and no vacation or sick time—the nominal number of business days in a year is 250. This means making 150 visits per year would require seeing *three* people every week. Granted, community colleges do not have the robust lists of major gift prospects that their four-year counterparts compile, but the point is that serious cultivation requires a serious time commitment. And, as noted earlier, the college president must play a significant role in soliciting a major gift. An individual who is ready to make a substantial donation deserves face time with the CEO.

Planned Giving.   Planned giving, sometimes called gift planning, refers to any major gift made during the donor's life or at death as part of an overall financial or estate plan. Planned gifts have existed for many years and account for today's billion-dollar endowments at many institutions like Harvard, Yale, and Princeton. Yet, community colleges tend to overlook the importance of this key vehicle, possibly because the payoff is not immediate. In addition, planned gifts can be difficult to solicit in the absence of a long history of annual giving. "Launching a planned giving program . . . just might be one of the most important things you will ever do for your college" (Klingaman, 2012, p. 211).

Planned giving options include bequests (giving property or cash through a will), endowment funds (establishing a permanent fund for a particular program or purpose), insurance (contributing an existing life insurance policy), and charitable gift annuities (transferring cash or property to the charity in exchange for a partial tax deduction and a lifetime stream of income), just to name a few. Bequests account for 80% of all planned gifts (Klingaman, 2012), and many times these gifts are a total surprise to the institution. (During our tenure at Oakton Community College, for example, the College's Educational Foundation enjoyed some $4 million in unexpected bequests from donors without a history of giving.)

Following the four-year college model, a handful of community colleges have legacy societies that recognize the donor's intention to support the institution through a will or other type of deferred gift (Wilmington Trust, 2013). Some of the most viable prospects for making a planned gift are within the institution, including current and retired faculty, current and retired staff, senior administrators, long-term foundation board members, and major donors with an impressive record of supporting the college. Websites of community colleges with legacy societies often provide prospective donors with detailed information on what these societies are and how individuals can participate. Examples include the legacy society websites for Joliet Junior College (2012) in Illinois, the Community College of Baltimore County (2014) in Maryland, and Bucks County Community College (2014) in Pennsylvania.

Special Events.   Many community colleges still rely on special events—especially galas and golf outings—to raise money for their institutions. While special events can be an important tool for donor cultivation and stewardship, development offices are beginning to recognize that the amount of preparation time required to pull off a successful event may not be worth the net results. In addition, the competition is fierce.

During any given month, dozens of charities sponsor events with the same format—silent and live auctions, raffles, open-bar and buffet, and some kind of "themed" entertainment.

In short, special events are synonymous with donor fatigue, sapping annual fund donations and preempting other fundraising strategies. A gala in March and a golf outing in September are a recipe for disaster for development offices with a limited pool of donors.

Community college fundraisers would be better served by redirecting the energy involved in planning and implementing a special event toward cultivating major donors. For example, Oakton Community College hosts an annual donor recognition banquet that provides the opportunity for donors to the Student Scholarship Fund to meet the scholarship recipients and hear their compelling stories. The evening squarely focuses on the mission of the college: to transform students' lives. The return on this $25,000 investment is remarkable; 45% of donations to the Scholarship Fund typically arrive within two weeks after the event, and some donors establish strong relationships with the students by offering internships or employment. These tangible results clearly trump galas and golf outings.

Online Strategies.   This discussion of philanthropic strategies in community colleges would not be complete without a nod to online giving. Already the country has witnessed the overwhelming response via social media to galvanize donor support during disasters like Hurricane Sandy and the earthquakes in Haiti and Japan. Four-year colleges and universities are now harnessing the power of social media for raising money. Florida State University, for example, recently launched a 36-hour online-only giving campaign that raised $186,000 from 1,100 donors; 90% of these donors had never given online and 380 were first-time contributors (Ware, 2012). Columbia University also recognized enormous success with a 24-hour "Columbia Giving Day" online appeal that brought in more than $6.8 million (Ware, 2013).

Tapping into this important new fundraising tool will require community colleges to build an online ambassador program so that supporters push out the message to their networks of friends. In addition, the institution's website must have the infrastructure in place to handle the volume of online gifts, and finally, the institution needs a full-time social media manager who can engage the volunteers working on behalf of the organization.

External Foundations

Although the fundraising strategies discussed above primarily target individuals or corporations, external or private-sector foundations are also important sources of financial support. This was underscored in the community college world when two major external foundations began funding community college programs. In 2004, the Lumina Foundation for Education committed substantial funds to launch Achieving the Dream, a national initiative to improve community college student success. Between 2004 and 2009, the Foundation invested more than $60 million in Achieving the Dream (Lumina Foundation, 2009). Several years later, the Bill and Melinda Gates Foundation pledged nearly $35 million over five years to improve graduation rates in community colleges through its Completion by Design (2014) initiative. Community college leaders took note, and "getting Gates Foundation funds" seemed to become the new benchmark for grants offices.

Nonetheless, according to the Foundation Center (2014a), 81,777 foundations in the United States gave just shy of $49 billion in 2011. Of that, $1.68 billion went to higher education (down from a high of $2.25 billion in 2007). Understanding how these foundations function is essential if community colleges are to be successful in their efforts to tap into this underused source of funding.

Types of Foundations.   Several categories of external foundations disburse funds to varying degrees for multiple purposes (see, e.g., Bailey & Browning, 2007). *Public foundations* obtain their funds from donations and disburse their funds through grants. They are viewed as public charitable organizations by the Internal Revenue Service and file annual "Form 990" returns that are accessible to the public. Many concentrate on a particular area of need such as child abuse, the environment, women's issues, hunger, and healthcare.

Community foundations are a form of public foundation that focus on a specific geographic region and concentrate on the area's economic, social, educational, or civic needs. Community colleges often find their local community foundation a primary source for program support, particularly in areas of workforce and economic development, low-income student needs, or other areas that would benefit the community at large.

Private foundations include independent, family, and corporate foundations. All file IRS 990-PF forms and must disburse 5% of their annual income each year. Trustees or directors make the funding decisions, and most of these foundations were created to fund specific activities or enterprises. Assets can be less than $100,000 or in the hundreds of millions.

Among the private foundations are *small family foundations*, which often have a distinct purpose determined by the original intent of the primary founder, or by family members who serve as the current directors. They may fund scholarships in a particular field, aid the local hospital, or contribute to a charitable organization in the area. They may be run more informally and be more approachable than large family foundations that have professional staffs, well-defined guidelines, and prescribed processes for application. Small family foundations may be a good source for endowing scholarships, providing equipment to set up a health or science laboratory, or funding arts activities and facilities.

Corporate foundations are also an important subset of private foundations. Different from corporate giving programs, they are separate legal organizations usually funded by the parent company and often follow the company's business interests. Their funding disbursements are disclosed to the public according to IRS regulations, and those seeking funds from corporate foundations must usually follow formal, prescribed application policies. Corporate foundations typically identify their funding interests on their websites and they may be quite specific. Examples include the Dollar General Literacy Foundation (2013), which helps "individuals learn to read, prepare for the GED, or learn English" (para. 2), and the American Honda Foundation established by the American Honda Motor Company (2014), which focuses on youth education with an emphasis on the environment, science, technology, engineering, and mathematics. On the other hand, *corporate giving* is private, and may include employee matching gifts and support programs that are not within the scope of the corporate foundation (Foundation Center, 2014c).

Best Practices.   Public, community, private, family, and corporate foundations are all potential sources of funding for community colleges, and a wealth of "how to" information exists on writing proposals, making contacts, and gaining funding through associations such as Foundation Center (http://foundationcenter.org/), the Council for Resource Development (http://crdnet.org/), professional grant organizations (e.g., the Grant Professionals Association), and books by the dozens (e.g., Bailey & Browning, 2007; Bauer, 2001; Browning, 2014). In addition, there are many helpful blogs, including "The Grant Advisors" (http://the-grant-advisors.com/) and "For Grant Writers Only" (http://blog.forgrantwritersonly.com/). Colleges can also contract with commercial grant search databases for a fee. When it comes to best practices for community colleges, the wisdom of dozens of professionals, shared over the course of decades in the field, is most useful. Key best practices are detailed next.

Make Fundraising Part of the College's Strategic Plan.   Before any website is accessed, any manual opened, or any phone call made, obtaining external foundation funding starts with a comprehensive vision of what the college hopes to accomplish in the next five or so years and how it hopes to get there. Application to an external foundation isn't an afterthought, as in, "Oh, maybe we could fund this program through the Y-Not Foundation. I hear they gave The College in the Next County money for lab equipment." Rather, foundations provide funding to entities that are capable, committed to the effort, have the structure and capacity to effectively manage the programs for which funding is obtained, and are fully cognizant of their needs and mission. In identifying the goals and objectives of the college, the strategic plan can pinpoint where additional funding is needed over the long term: general operations, enhanced programming, staffing, new equipment, improvements to facilities, and the like. Designate priorities and analyze the costs that will be incurred versus the benefits and need for the funding. This in turn drives the development of a comprehensive funding plan that gives direction and unity to the effort.

It Takes a Village.   Gather a diverse team to prepare background information needed in the development of a proposal that will be sent to an external agency. Involve staff not only from the finance office, but also from college advancement, resource development, institutional effectiveness, institutional research, marketing, academic and student affairs, and workforce development. The extensive data needed for any proposal will need to come from numerous sources. Faculty members may have anecdotal stories about student experiences that might give a face to a project that the college is attempting to support. In addition, analytics may come from institutional research, an economic impact statement from the workforce development staff, a prospective budget from the grant writer, accounting director, and academic dean. A widespread group will also identify potential collaborators within the wider community who can help make the case for funding. Prospective employers, local businesses or community organizations, and social service agencies may all play a role in the eventual proposal.

The advantage of using a team becomes even more apparent when the time arrives to approach a potential foundation. Personal contact and relationship building are integral to developing the knowledge and understanding needed between a potential funder and the grant seeker. Before submitting a proposal, someone needs to talk to the funder. The best spokesperson for the college may not be the person expected to implement the proposed activity or the one who will write the proposal. As is often the case when approaching individual donors, it may be important for the college president and board chair to make the contact with external foundations. An alliance of community, business, and college personnel may have several contacts at a particular foundation that can ease the initial communication. As with government grants, foundations often require colleges to implement funded projects in partnership with other community stakeholders; in those cases proposals will be more favorably received if these partnerships are in place from the project's conception.

Tackle Sustainability First.   As the project begins to evolve, sustainability should be among the first issues that are addressed. The statement, "Additional funding will be sought from various external sources in 3–4 years," will be interpreted by external foundations as, "We have no idea how we're going to keep this project going if you don't give us more money." This is a death sentence to the project. A project written into the college's strategic plan, with clearly defined funding requirements and identified sources of funds beyond initial private monies, is more likely to receive the attention of funders. It will also help the college determine whether the program can be institutionalized with acceptable costs, or needs to be restructured after initial funding to fit into the budget. For instance, a student support project that requires five additional staff members, initially funded through external sources, has little chance of continuation unless the college can show exactly how those new positions will be financed. The college might then choose to use institutional funds for that project and ask the external foundation to help fund purchase of "start-up" equipment that requires only minimal maintenance.

Do the Research.   It would seem axiomatic that researching prospective foundations is essential, but it is so often stressed by funding professionals that it apparently needs repeating. A former Foundation Center employee noted that mass mailings of letters of inquiry are a sure way to lose any chance with a potential funder. The Foundation Center (2014b) cautions:

> Contacting a grant maker with a phone call or written proposal without having researched it first often wastes time and effort for you and the funder. Even worse, not doing your homework can make you seem unprofessional, which can undermine your nonprofit's reputation. (para. 1)

Public and private foundations have missions, and they generally post those missions, often listed as "areas of funding interest," on their websites. Directories of foundations are available, and web-based databases have simplified the process. IRS forms 990 and 990-PF filed by foundations are publicly available and also tell whom the foundation funds. It's possible to learn whether a particular foundation funds community colleges, in what geographic areas, in what subject areas, and at what level of funding. Background research on foundations also reveals what they don't fund and when they tend to make funding decisions. Proposal guidelines are posted with information on the timing of funding cycles, whether foundations accept unsolicited proposals, and how the proposals should be written and submitted. Prospect research is both time consuming and imperative.

Is There a Fit?   Although it is essential to understand the implications of a foundation's mission and funding priorities, it is even more important to know whether that mission fits with the college's priorities. There are costs to fundraising that are not always apparent. Foundation grants, like government grants, come with strings attached. Just as a corporate foundation mirrors the company's interests, public and private foundation boards also seek outcomes that match their priorities. With the Gates Foundation's $472 million funding to higher education (Parry, Field, & Supiano, 2013), its effort to accelerate completion is perhaps most well known, but it is hardly the only foundation attempting to alter policy or effect change according to its objectives. In turning to external resources for funding, the college has to consider a number of issues: Can the college meet a foundation's requirements without changing its own objectives? Will foundation funding push a college in a direction for which it is not yet ready? Is, for example, funding from a utility company that engages in "fracking" acceptable to a college with an activist environmental community? Will a community foundation require data substantiating the progress of low-income students in a way the college does not track—and what would be the cost to add that tracking? Is funding for adult education tied to a type of assessment program the college does not use?

Go Local. It may be appealing to dive right in with the well-known, massive national foundations that seem to have boundless funds to distribute and could provide great publicity for the college. But building successful foundation partners is more likely to happen locally with nearby family, corporate, and community foundations. Already familiar with your institution, these are the funders with whom long-lasting connections can be established. They are more likely to understand local needs and will have a mutual interest in ensuring the best possible outcomes for the project.

Keep at It. A grant blog headline recently proclaimed, "There's No Crying in Fundraising" (Klimko, 2014). But there definitely will be rejections and disappointment. Grant developers often refer to a "rule of three": It takes three times before an application is funded. A proposal to a private sector foundation is no different. If the request for funding has been rejected, contact the individual with whom the college has established a relationship. Ask for help in understanding how the project can be improved so that it might be resubmitted successfully. The time spent in building contacts before submitting the proposal will prove its value.

Conclusion

Although late in coming to community colleges, resource development programs remain more critical than ever in the face of unprecedented economic challenges facing higher education. Arguably the most important factor in ensuring success is to have an institutional commitment—and a president willing to advance the efforts of development and grants offices. Successful fundraising programs require a team orientation—a college-wide responsibility that includes roles for administrators, faculty, staff, governing board members, and members of the foundation board. In the words of Neil Kreisel and Vanessa Patterson (2013), "As champions of our beloved community colleges, fundraisers must stand up for the millions of students depending on us to keep the doors of opportunity open for them" (para. 13).

References

American Honda Motor Company. (2014). *American Honda Foundation.* Retrieved from http://corporate.honda.com/america/philanthropy.aspx?id=ahf

Bailey, L., & Browning, B. A. (2007). *Winning strategies for developing proposals and managing grants* (3rd ed.). Washington, DC: Thompson Publishing.

Bauer, D. G. (2001). *How to evaluate and improve your grants effort* (2nd ed.). Westport, CT: Oryx Press.

Browning, B. A. (2014). *Grant writing for dummies* (5th ed.). Hoboken, NJ: Wiley.

Bucks County Community College. (2014). *Planned giving—Tyler Legacy Society.* Retrieved from http://www.bucks.edu/about/foundation/plannedgiving-tylerlegacy society/

Century Foundation Task Force on Preventing Community Colleges from Becoming Separate and Unequal. (2013). *Bridging the higher education divide: Strengthening community colleges and restoring the American dream.* Retrieved from the Century Foundation website: http://tcf.org/assets/downloads/20130523-Bridging _the_Higher_Education_Divide-REPORT-ONLY.pdf

Community College of Baltimore County. (2014). *CCBC Legacy Society.* Retrieved from http://www.legacy.vg/ccbcmd/giving/2.html

Completion by Design. (2014). *About us.* Retrieved from http://completionby design.org/about-us

Council for Aid to Education. (2013). *2013 voluntary support of education.* New York, NY: Author.

Dollar General Literacy Foundation. (2013). *Literacy grant programs.* Retrieved from http://www2.dollargeneral.com/dgliteracy/Pages/grant_programs.aspx

Double the Donation. (2014). *Matching gift statistics: Matching gift key figures and industry trends.* Retrieved from https://doublethedonation.com/matching-grant -resources/matching-gift-statistics/

Flahaven, B., & Glover, T. (2010, February). *Community college foundations: An analysis of a survey conducted by the Council for the Advancement and Support of Education.* Retrieved from Council for the Advancement and Support of Education website: http://www.case.org/Documents/WhitePapers/CCF_WhitePaper.pdf

Foundation Center. (2014a). *Foundation stats.* Retrieved from http://data .foundationcenter.org/#/fc1000/subject:education/all/total/trends:amount/2011

Foundation Center. (2014b). *Knowledge base. How do I approach a foundation and build a successful grantee-funder relationship?* Retrieved from Grant Space website: http://grantspace.org/Tools/Knowledge-Base/Funding-Resources/Foundations /approaching-foundations

Foundation Center. (2014c). *Knowledge base. What is the difference between a company-sponsored foundation and a corporate direct giving program?* Retrieved from Grant Space website: http://grantspace.org/Tools/Knowledge-Base/Funding-Resources /Foundations/corporate-foundations-vs-giving-programs

Joliet Junior College. (2012). *Donors and giving clubs.* Retrieved from http://www.jjc .edu/foundation/Pages/list-donors.aspx

Jones, P. M. (2010). *Exploring factors that impact success in community college fundraising* (New Century Series Resource Paper No. 18). Washington, DC: Council for Resource Development. Retrieved from http://titlestand.com/ebook/ebook?id =10017462&ts=1#/0

Klimko, F. (2014). There's no crying in fundraising [The Grant Advisors web log post]. Retrieved from http://the-grant-advisors.com/2014/04/30/theres-no -crying-in-fundraising/#more-652

Klingaman, S. (2012). *Fundraising strategies for community colleges: The definitive guide for advancement.* Sterling, VA: Stylus.

Kreisel, N., & Patterson, V. (2013, July 8). How community colleges can help themselves. *The Chronicle of Higher Education.* Retrieved from http://chronicle.com/article /How-Community-Colleges-Can/140121/

Lumina Foundation. (2009, December 3). *Achieving the dream: Community colleges count announces William Trueheart as CEO* [Press release]. Retrieved from http://www.luminafoundation.org/newsroom/news_releases/2009-12-03.html

Parry, M., Field, K., & Supiano, B. (2013, July 14). The Gates effect. *Chronicle of Higher Education.* Retrieved from http://chronicle.com/article/The-Gates-Effect/140323/

Teahen, R., Guy, K., & Byl, B. (2012). *The X factor: Does your foundation board have it?* (New Century Series Resource Paper No. 22). Washington, DC: Council for Resource Development. Retrieved from http://titlestand.com/ebook/ebook?id=10020265&ts =1#/0

Ware, J. (2012, February 17). Florida State wins big with 36-hour online fundraising campaign [The Social Side of Giving web log post]. Retrieved from http://justinjware.com/2012/02/17/florida-state-wins-big-with-36-hour-online-fundraising-campaign/

Ware, J. (2013, January 18). Online ambassadors help Columbia reach $6.8 million in 24 hours [The Social Side of Giving web log post]. Retrieved from http://justinjware.com/2013/01/18/online-ambassadors-help-columbia-reach-6-8-million-in-24-hours/

Wilmington Trust. (2013). *Community colleges: Insights on fundraising and endowment strategies.* Retrieved from http://www.wilmingtontrust.com/repositories/wtc_sitecontent/PDF/2013_Community_College_Article.pdf

CARLEE DRUMMER *is the president of Quinebaug Valley Community College in Danielson, CT.*

ROXANN MARSHBURN *is the director of grants and alternative funding at Oakton Community College, Des Plaines, IL.*

NEW DIRECTIONS FOR COMMUNITY COLLEGES • DOI: 10.1002/cc

This chapter explores the concept of entrepreneurial waves, with a special focus on the "third wave" of entrepreneurial ventures: alternative means of funding programs and services in light of continued reductions in public financial support and as an approach to building strong and sustainable relationships with external constituencies. The chapter also explores the leadership characteristics necessary to create and sustain a culture of entrepreneurship.

Entrepreneurship: The College as a Business Enterprise

Brent D. Cejda, Michael R. Jolley

In a 2003 *New Directions for Community Colleges* chapter, Milliron, de los Santos, and Browning pointed to a community college president who noted, "We will soon need to call ourselves publicly assisted colleges instead of publicly supported colleges because of our shrinking fixed allocations from state and local sources" (p. 90). This reflects the decline in state funding for community colleges that began in the early 1980s and continued into the 21st century (Roessler, Katsinas, & Hardy, 2006). The continued reductions of traditional financial resources have led community college administrators to seek out alternative means of funding, primarily through collaborative agreements with local and regional businesses (AACC, 2012; Barr & McClellan, 2011; Center for Community College Policy, 2000).

Milliron et al. (2003) incorporated Toffler's (1989) concept of the third wave to describe transformation and change in the community college movement. In short, Toffler emphasized transitions along three major waves: from the agrarian age to the industrial age to the information age. Similarly, Milliron et al. contended that community colleges also change according to societal trends. They asserted that the first wave was the rise of the comprehensive community college and that the second wave involved entrepreneurial approaches, including a large focus on workforce development. The third wave was posited as an era in which community colleges entered "into full partnerships on the economic and educational landscape and develop[ed] the relationships necessary to support our institutions more fully on the road ahead" (Milliron et al., 2003, p. 82).

In approaching this chapter, we placed our focus on two primary areas. First, we sought to identify the distinguishing features of "third-wave" community colleges that have become institutions that create an environment that fosters sustainable, long-term economic and educational initiatives. Second, we sought to determine the role of leadership in moving entrepreneurial initiatives into the core of the institutional culture. To accomplish these purposes, we relied upon colleagues across the community college spectrum to identify institutions they would describe as entrepreneurial community colleges. On the basis of feedback from selected staff members of the American Association of Community Colleges (AACC) and the board members of two AACC-affiliated councils, we compiled an initial list of 12 community colleges. We then used a snowball sampling technique, asking representatives of these 12 institutions to identify other community colleges they would characterize as entrepreneurial. This led to the identification of eight additional institutions.

Our first step was to contact individuals from these 20 institutions to determine entrepreneurial activities in line with the third-wave concept. We then interviewed 15 individuals in an attempt to identify the role of leadership in moving entrepreneurial initiatives into the core of the institutional culture. The following sections (a) note how the activities of the 20 identified colleges reflect the first, second, and third waves depicted by Milliron et al.; (b) provide examples of entrepreneurial activities from two of the identified colleges that come close to reflecting third-wave work; (c) describe the organizational features of community colleges that approach third-wave work; and (d) detail the role of leadership at these institutions.

Entrepreneurship in Community Colleges

Entrepreneurship is a common term in the community college vocabulary. We make this statement on the basis of the fact that no one we contacted or interviewed asked us to define what we meant by entrepreneurship. Yet we found differing interpretations. A few of our identified institutions matched the first-wave thinking of the comprehensive community college in that they were expanding programs to meet their missions. To these institutions, entrepreneurship existed through the addition of programs. Increasing dual-credit offerings with high schools, adding additional sites to offer courses or increasing online offerings, or implementing innovative programs to increase the job preparation and workforce development mission (e.g., technology programs in alternative or renewable energy) serve as examples of continuing first-wave activity. A second group of identified institutions were primarily involved in second-wave activities of expanding contract training or business partnerships. To these institutions, entrepreneurship existed through the identification of needs of existing

NEW DIRECTIONS FOR COMMUNITY COLLEGES • DOI: 10.1002/cc

business and industry in their service areas and the development of programs to meet these needs. Most often these offerings were noncredit: the programs were offered outside of the regular college calendar and were offered at the business/industry location.

We found that a distinction existed in a third group of institutions. Activities noted earlier as first or second wave focused primarily on immediately bringing additional resources to the community colleges. Third-wave thinking considers the impact of community college activities from an economic and community development perspective and places importance on the sustainability of entrepreneurial activities. Outside entities (e.g., school districts, business and industry, governmental agencies) are considered as potential long-term partners, not simply for the short-term benefit of additional revenue for an extra course or customized training session.

We do not mean to indicate a "pecking order" distinction among our examples of the respective waves. In fact, a significant finding in our examination is that the community colleges that fit in the third wave—those that view entrepreneurship as sustainable, long-term economic and educational initiatives—followed a developmental process and progression. Simply put, no institution jumped immediately into the third wave.

Third-Wave Examples

Our interviews revealed a number of institutions planning or implementing third-wave ventures. Multiple individuals made mention of programs in place at Kirkwood Community College and Walla Walla Community College. As the most referenced institutions, examples of these respective community colleges illustrate a strong commitment to third-wave thinking as described by Milliron and his colleagues.

Kirkwood Community College.   This institution has long been known for its partnership with AEGON USA, an insurance company. As detailed in *The Entrepreneurial Community College* (Roueche & Jones, 2005), this partnership began in 1985 when Kirkwood began providing a customized training program to AEGON. One outgrowth of the partnership, as detailed by Roueche and Jones, is that AEGON funded the construction of a $1.6 million facility for business education and information technology on the Kirkwood campus in 2002. This example illustrates the move from the second wave, providing customized training, to the third wave, where the entrepreneurial activity results in a benefit to the broader student constituency.

This one example, however, does not fully present the complexity of the third wave at Kirkwood. The institution uses the heading "strategic partnerships" to point out that "Many of Kirkwood's greatest accomplishments have come from working with a host of private and public entities for the good of our entire area" (Kirkwood Community College, 2013, para. 1). Kirkwood has continued working with AEGON USA, but partnerships with other business and industry entities exist. For example, Diamond V Mills, Inc., an animal nutrition company, has a research and innovation center on the Kirkwood campus. Kirkwood has also expanded client-specific contract training by developing Kirkwood Training and Outreach Services (KTOS). In addition to a physical center that provides meeting and training spaces, KTOS has developed a menu of broad-based training and other services for area business and industry and has administered state-based Jobs Training Programs. The college has also partnered with city and county agencies on the creation of a shared emergency operations center and with local real estate developers to provide privately owned housing for Kirkwood students adjacent to the campus.

Walla Walla Community College.   One of the primary reasons that Walla Walla Community College is known as an entrepreneurial entity is its viticulture program. Murphy (2014) provides a representative description of the program, pointing out that in 2000 a local group of vintners worked with Walla Walla Community College to create a viticulture program. The progression of this effort, fueled by $5 million from the wine industry and other private sources, culminated in the creation of College Cellars of Walla Walla, a teaching winery located at the Center for Enology and Viticulture on the campus of Walla Walla Community College. The Center houses classrooms and a wine analysis laboratory. The award-winning vineyard and fully operational commercial winery, including a tasting room, provide graduates with job skills for this growing industry. In 2000, when the program began, there were 20 wineries in the region. The program is credited as a key reason the Walla Walla area now has 140 wineries.

As with the AEGON example at Kirkwood, the viticulture program does not itself illustrate the complexity of the third wave at Walla Walla. What is rarely mentioned in descriptions of the wine program is the economic downturn that occurred in the late 1990s when Walla Walla lost a sawmill and a cannery. The Walla Walla president indicated that as a result of the loss of industry, there was a need for the college to reinvent itself (Jacobs, 2014). The wine initiative was one of the first attempts at reinvention. A corollary to College Cellars is the Walla Walla Incubators. A project funded by the state and the Port of Walla Walla, the incubators represent a $1.9 million investment to provide an incubator site dedicated to entrepreneurs who are launching wineries. A culinary program, also located at the Center for Enology and Viticulture, has recently been added to complement the viticulture program. Additional steps in reinvention include a wind-turbine technology program and a tractor repair program, both supporting business and industry in the greater region served by the college.

These two examples demonstrate three primary points about the third wave of entrepreneurial activity in community colleges. Third-wave entrepreneurial activity not only provides additional revenue for the community college but also provides benefits to the greater community that the college serves. Third-wave entrepreneurial activity is systematic, purposeful, and involves many people and entities. Finally, third-wave entrepreneurial activity is evolutionary and includes components of first- and second-wave work. The third-wave community college can be viewed as an enterprise that focuses on developed relationships that contribute to the sustainability of the college and the broader community the institution serves.

Moving Toward a Third-Wave Culture

For many community colleges, entrepreneurial activities exist outside of traditional college credit programs and are often placed in their own divisions and staffed with separate administrators and faculty (Van Noy, Jacobs, Korey, Bailey, & Hughes, 2008). This "separate" organizational structure reflects the second-wave emphasis on workforce development and customized training, often offered through noncredit programs. Jacobs and Teahen (1997) coined the term "Shadow College" to describe an organizational structure that allows the institution to be responsive to the needs of constituencies and to shadow regular programming, creating an institution within an institution. Grubb, Badway, Bell, Bragg, and Russman (1997) point out that no one term is adequate, but label the shadow college the "entrepreneurial college," explaining that "this term better captures the entrepreneurial spirit and market-oriented drive behind these activities [of the shadow college]" (p. 2).

Morest (2006) points out that some community colleges have integrated noncredit and credit programs for two particular reasons: to take advantage of operational efficiencies and encourage cooperation across programs and to facilitate mobility of students across noncredit and credit offerings. The individuals we interviewed at third-wave institutions, however, did not stress organizational structure. Third-wave thinking moves beyond the structural addition of a shadow college, attempting to transform the college culture and develop an entrepreneurial spirit throughout the organization. One community college president explained:

> For a number of years we have had what I would refer to as entrepreneurial strategies or entrepreneurial ventures. These have often been stand-alone projects, with a small group of individuals involved. Our recent efforts have been to move to an entrepreneurial culture that permeates the institution. Our entrepreneurial ventures are not totally customized training or other noncredit offerings. The entire institution needs to be responsive and innovative. Credit or noncredit doesn't matter.

Multiple reasons to establish an entrepreneurial culture that included both credit and noncredit offerings were provided by the individuals we interviewed. The most common reason was funding. Many states provide reduced or no funding for noncredit programming. Moreover, state funding has declined, but is still predominately based on credit hour production. Collaborations and partnerships with high schools, other community colleges, and four-year institutions were identified by a number of respondents as entrepreneurial activities, and were most often credit-based activities. A number of respondents also referenced cocurricular activities such as service learning and student research, often initiated by individual faculty members, as another reason to develop a culture throughout the community college instead of isolating entrepreneurial initiatives. A common characteristic in our interview responses was the importance of institutionalizing entrepreneurial activities. A vice president emphasized:

> I need innovation to be institutionalized, not individualized. When only one faculty member is involved in an innovative project you do not have a sustainable effort because the project would end if that faculty member left the institution. I strive to get buy-in from broader divisions for innovative practices— the entire science division for example—rather than from just one chemistry professor.

A Strengthened Steering Core

In his examination of entrepreneurial universities, Clark (1998) identified a strengthened administrative core as mandatory if an institution was to move toward an innovative, responsive mode. The strengthened administrative core provides greater institutional capacity to provide direction and to steer the organization. Clark emphasized that the development of a strengthened steering core did not take any one organizational form and often included aspects unique to the respective institutions. Responses from the community college leaders we interviewed supported this emphasis. One community college president explained:

> We did not change our organizational structure, but I did form a new council that includes representatives from our academic units as well as continuing education and community education. The focus of this council is discussing opportunities that exist to develop new programs or introduce innovation into existing programs. A result is that many of the faculty, who most often worked in only the academic programs, are now active in continuing and community education.

Another president shared the following:

> Several of our vocational programs have strong advisory boards for their specific programs. But the institution as a whole needed to expand the concept of advisory boards. We now have an advisory board that is comprised of

representatives of the chamber of commerce and economic development corporations in communities we serve as well as an advisory board of all of the school districts in our service area. We have expanded our ability to identify potential opportunities and partnerships from specific programs to the institution as a whole.

Among institutions with a steering core, Clark found that the administration has worked with the more traditional academic enterprise to fuse entrepreneurial values with traditional academic values. Risser's (2007) study of three entrepreneurial community colleges found a cooperative faculty–administrative relationship in support of new initiatives. Our interview participants agreed that cooperation across boundaries was essential, but also stressed the importance of clear lines of authority.

Regardless of how the strengthened core was formed, Clark (1998) identified the common practice of individuals within the core to continuously seek resources for the institution as a whole. The community college leaders we interviewed provide support for this finding. One president shared:

> The members of our leadership council do not wait passively, hoping for state funding to return to previous levels. We look externally at any and all opportunities for new revenue streams.

As a result of steering the entire institution toward new streams of revenue, respondents affirmed the third-wave aspect of institutional sustainability. One participant indicated:

> It isn't simply that the contract activities with businesses help support the credit programs in our business division. Our division helps support programs in other divisions of the institution. We are dependent on courses in other divisions in order to offer our certificate and degree programs. Other divisions support what we do instructionally; we provide them with some financial support. Without the other divisions we would no longer be a comprehensive community college.

This observation, and others, indicates that the managerial core seeks not only to secure funding for new activities and programs but to use these additional resources to support or enhance existing programs that are valuable to the organizational mission but may not have similar funding opportunities. As a result, the managerial core provides the institution with resources to meet two competing components of the community college mission, providing access to postsecondary education and meeting the needs of business and industry.

The Role of Leadership

Kanter (2011) stressed, "The best CEOs do it. Effective entrepreneurs do it. Middle managers who become change agents do it" (para. 1). The "it" Kanter refers to is convening: bringing groups together to tackle big issues and commit to action. McKeon (2013) points to the community college as a uniquely designed entity with the potential to act as the convener to generate meaningful advances in economic development initiatives. The power to convene is based on the office, not the person (Carlson, 2006). The individuals we interviewed identified convening as a primary role of leaders in developing full partnerships in their communities; holding a leadership position in the community college provided the power to convene. Several presidents indicated that while their institutions have been identified as catalysts, the activity that influenced change or action was convening.

Regardless of the term used, all respondents indicated the importance of convening educational, business, industry, civic, and governmental entities together in order to develop the relationships necessary to realize an entrepreneurial culture and secure greater levels of broad-based support. This points to an important corollary for convening, i.e., creating processes to identify community needs, potential partnerships, and other entrepreneurial opportunities. The community college presidents we interviewed indicated the importance of external relations in their leadership roles. Often they provide multiple opportunities for senior- and mid-level leaders to interact with external entities and additional opportunities for faculty and staff to showcase themselves and their programs. Senior-level leaders we interviewed referenced the opportunities presidents had provided for them and, in turn, the opportunities they provided for mid-level leaders and faculty members. In the words of one president:

> My role is to organize our leadership team and hire qualified people. I've learned it is best to then turn it over to them and become a facilitator and motivator. I need to provide opportunities for the leadership team and for our faculty and staff on the front line, those who actually do the work, to interact with our constituencies so that the innovative mindset becomes more apparent throughout our community college.

The individuals we interviewed pointed to the development of a communication strategy and serving as an effective communicator as an additional important leadership role. Senior leaders need to be effective communicators in order to convene disparate groups and to establish strong external relations, but also to communicate internally to mid-level administrators, faculty, and staff at the community college. Strategies to communicate effectively and efficiently both internally and externally are important for maintaining broad-based support throughout the service area as well as at the state and regional level. Two key points emerged when respondents were asked to be more specific about communication. The comments of one president emphasize the first point regarding internal communication:

> A key to increased innovative activity at our institution was making sure that everyone understood that innovation requires a certain amount of risk taking and that some initiatives will not be successful. I felt that we had only individuals attempting entrepreneurial activity because the collective whole did not realize that we needed, and valued, innovation and few people were willing to take any risks. As we have improved the understanding of the importance of entrepreneurial activity we now see groups working together to develop creative responses and programs.

Another president elaborated the second point of external communication by indicating:

> Our early efforts were essentially programs and projects to bring additional revenue to the institution. It was important for us to make sure that the school districts, businesses, and community organizations that we work with understood that we were interested in full partnerships; in making sure that we built long-term relationships that are win-win, not zero-sum. We spent a considerable amount of time designing an external communication strategy and now find that we are sought out as a partner.

A final specific role of leadership is to work with the board of trustees. One president confided that, in large part, the entrepreneurial nature of the community college stemmed from a board of trustees known to encourage and support innovation. Thus, the board did not need to be convinced. Another respondent indicated the leadership role of garnering support from the board. Without board support, leaders expressed doubt that more community colleges can move to the third wave.

Final Observations

As indicated in the introduction to this chapter, community colleges have experienced changes that can be described as waves influenced by societal demands. Community colleges in the third wave are engaged in partnerships that promote educational, community, and economic development for the long-term sustainability of their regions and, in turn, their institutions. Descriptions of innovative and entrepreneurial activities from the community college leaders we interviewed suggest that in the third wave, colleges move beyond isolated activities that bring additional resources to the institution. Instead, they enter into fuller partnerships that create win-win outcomes for the community college and for the broader constituencies the community college serves. The projects undertaken at Kirkwood Community College and Walla Walla Community College are examples. Those projects involve specific businesses and industries, support the broader needs of business and industry, and partner with governmental, civic, economic, and educational organizations.

Our interviews with community college leaders revealed that, regardless of the organizational structure, these and other institutions in the third wave have developed a culture that embraces and values innovative and entrepreneurial approaches. This culture is supported and maintained by a steering core of individuals who continually seek new partnerships and opportunities to both support new programs and enhance existing programs. Additional programs that continue the comprehensive mission of the community college, customized and contract training that meets the needs of business and industry, and activities that promote economic development and sustainability of the community and the college are all components of the third wave.

Leadership roles in third-wave community colleges focus on the power of convening, of bringing together groups to address common issues. Most certainly one issue is how community colleges replace revenues lost through declining state resources. Through efforts to support the sustainability of their service areas, respondents indicate similar support for the sustainability of the community colleges and their comprehensive missions. Creating a system to monitor the external environment and the development of quality external relations were identified as corollary roles of leaders. An important skill in facilitating the entrepreneurial culture is effective communication. Both internal and external communication strategies are crucial to maintaining relationships and in securing support from the board of trustees.

We must point out, however, that no one we interviewed conveyed the thought that they were riding the crest of the third wave. Time and again, participants in the interviews not only spoke of the progress that had been made but also pointed to the continuing uncertainty of their futures. In surfing terms, community colleges need to continue shredding the third wave to aggressively pursue entrepreneurial activities that benefit and contribute to the long-term sustainability of the communities they serve and provide greater support for the institution. Otherwise the danger remains of a wipe out.

References

AACC. (2012, April). *Reclaiming the American dream: A report from the 21st-Century Commission on the Future of Community Colleges*. Retrieved from http://www.insidehighered.com/sites/default/server_files/files/21stCentReport.pdf

Barr, M. J., & McClellan, G. S. (2011). *Budgets and financial management in higher education*. San Francisco, CA: Jossey-Bass.

Carlson, C. (2006). Using political power to convene. *National Civic Review, 95*(3), 57–60.

Center for Community College Policy. (2000). *State funding for community colleges: A 50-state survey*. Denver, CO: Education Commission of the States.

Clark, B. R. (1998). *Creating entrepreneurial universities: Organizational pathways of transformation*. Guilford, Surrey, UK: Biddles.

Grubb, W. N., Badway, N., Bell, D., Bragg, D., & Russman, M. (1997, June). *Workforce, economic, and community development. The changing landscape of the entrepreneurial community college*. Retrieved from Community College Resource Center, Teachers College, Columbia University website: http://ccrc.tc.columbia.edu/publications/workforce-economic-and-community-development.html

Jacobs, J. (2014, May 23). *Walla Walla: Fewer dropouts, more degrees*. Retrieved from Community College Spotlight website: http://communitycollegespotlight.org/content/walla-walla-fewer-dropouts-degrees_16872/

Jacobs, J., & Teahen, R. C. (1997). The shadow college and NCA accreditation: A conceptual framework. *NCA Quarterly, 71*(4), 472–478.

Kanter, R. M. (2011, September 19). *Bill Clinton and how to use convening power*. Retrieved from Harvard Business Review website: http://blogs.hbr.org/2011/09/bill-clinton-and-how-to-use-co/

Kirkwood Community College. (2013). *Strategic partnerships*. Retrieved from Kirkwood Community College website: http://www.kirkwood.edu/site/index.php?p=25508

McKeon, T. K. (2013). A college's role in developing and supporting an entrepreneurship ecosystem. *Journal of Higher Education Outreach and Engagement, 17*(3), 85–89.

Milliron, M. D., de los Santos, G. E., & Browning, B. (2003). Feels like the third wave: The rise of fundraising in the community college. In M. D. Milliron, G. E. de los Santos, & B. Browning (Eds.), *New Directions for Community Colleges: No. 124. Successful approaches to fundraising and development* (pp. 81–93). San Francisco, CA: Jossey-Bass.

Morest, V. S. (2006). Double vision: How the attempt to balance multiple missions is shaping the future of community colleges. In T. Bailey & V. S. Morest (Eds.), *Defending the community college equity agenda* (pp. 28–50). Baltimore, MD: Johns Hopkins University Press.

Murphy, C. (2014, April). *How to build a skilled workforce*. Retrieved from http://www.inc.com/magazine/201404/cait-murphy/how-to-build-a-skilled-workforce.html

Risser, B. G. (2007). *Faculty governance at the entrepreneurial community college* (Doctoral dissertation). Retrieved from http://repository.upenn.edu/dissertations/AAI3255864. (Paper AAI3255864)

Roessler, B., Katsinas, S., & Hardy, D. (2006). *The downward spiral of state funding for community colleges, and its impact on rural community colleges* (Policy Brief). Meridian, MS: University of Alabama Education Policy Center for the Mid-South Partnership for Rural Community Colleges.

Roueche, J. E., & Jones, B. R. (2005). *The entrepreneurial community college*. Washington, DC: Community College Press.

Toffler, A. (1989). *The third wave*. New York, NY: Bantam.

Van Noy, M., Jacobs, J., Korey, S., Bailey, T., & Hughes, K. L. (2008). *Noncredit enrollment in workforce education: State policies and community college practices*. Retrieved from AACC | Reports and White Papers website: http://www.aacc.nche.edu/Publications/Reports/Documents/noncredit.pdf

Brent D. Cejda *is a professor and chair of the Educational Administration Department at the University of Nebraska-Lincoln.*

Michael R. Jolley *is an instructional design technology specialist and a doctoral student in educational leadership and higher education at the University of Nebraska-Lincoln.*

New Directions for Community Colleges • DOI: 10.1002/cc

9

In this age of educational accountability, there is an increasing emphasis on assessment and institutional effectiveness, not only in the academic arena but also in other aspects of community college operation, such as fiscal health and stability, revenue generation, resource allocation, facilities, workforce development, and community enrichment services. This chapter describes the challenge of effectively assessing community college financial services and budgets as well as internal and external standards and benchmarks developed to measure institutional fiscal health and the allocation of resources (e.g., reserve fund amounts, deferred maintenance, and bond ratings).

Assessing Financial Health in Community Colleges

Trudy H. Bers, Ronald B. Head

Assessment has played a key role in higher education for several decades now, and most community college faculty and staff are familiar with assessing student learning outcomes and evaluating academic program effectiveness. Although this assessment focus has been in place since the late 1980s and has generated a great deal of attention on assessment within the academic side of the house, the fiscal rollercoaster that has characterized funding for community colleges in the past decade has increased pressure for colleges to document their fiscal health, not only "accounting" for revenues and expenditures, but also demonstrating prudent and efficient use of scarce resources. Every aspect of a community college has come under increased scrutiny, from academics to student services and from facilities to finances.

Assessing the financial effectiveness of a community college, however, is still something of a mystery to most in the community college world, and the literature is strangely silent when it comes to this. Indeed, using the electronic search engine One Search, a recent query of the literature returned 671 sources when the search terms *community college* and *institutional effectiveness* were applied; when the term *finance* was added, only 41 sources were returned and none of these dealt specifically with financial assessment (the word *finance* simply appeared somewhere within the documents). This

NEW DIRECTIONS FOR COMMUNITY COLLEGES, no. 168, Winter 2014 © 2014 Wiley Periodicals, Inc.
Published online in Wiley Online Library (wileyonlinelibrary.com) • DOI: 10.1002/cc.20124

chapter describes some of the driving forces behind the need for increased financial accountability and presents some of the methods for determining the financial health of community colleges.

Demands for Fiscal Accountability in Community Colleges

Regional accreditation is one of the major driving forces requiring community colleges to demonstrate effectiveness in all of their operations and services. Indeed, the very concept of institutional effectiveness was developed in the mid-1980s in response to regional accreditation, and today all six regional accreditors have adopted standards for determining fiscal health (Ewell, 2011; Head, 2011; Head & Johnson, 2011). Two examples are provided here, one from the Southern Association of Colleges and Schools Commission on Colleges (SACSCOC) and the other from the Higher Learning Commission (HLC).

Each member institution of the SACSCOC is required to have "a sound financial base and demonstrated financial stability to support the mission of the institution and the scope of its programs and services" (SACSCOC, 2012, p. 20). To demonstrate this, institutions must submit to the commission (a) institutional audits, (b) statements of unrestricted net assets, and (c) annual budget statements. Additionally, SACSCOC has established the following standards:

- The institution's recent financial history demonstrates financial stability. (*Financial stability*)
- The institution audits financial aid programs as required by federal and state regulations. (*Financial aid audits*)
- The institution exercises appropriate control over all its financial resources. (*Control of finances*)
- The institution maintains financial control over externally funded or sponsored research and programs. (*Control of sponsored research/external funds*) (SACSCOC, 2012, p. 32)

The HLC has established five criteria for accreditation, the fifth of which relates to resources, planning, and institutional effectiveness. Among the core components of Criterion 5 are the requirements that "The institution has the fiscal and human resources and physical and technological infrastructure sufficient to support its operations wherever and however programs are delivered" and that "The institution has a well-developed process in place for budgeting and for monitoring expense" (Higher Learning Commission, 2013, p. 5). The HLC also expects institutions to be forward-thinking, as one of the planning requirements is that "Institutional plans anticipate the possible impact of fluctuations in the institution's sources of revenue, such as enrollment, the economy, and state support" (Higher

Learning Commission, 2013, p. 6). Finally, public institutions seeking HLC accreditation must submit specific indicators of fiscal health, ratios that have become common across higher education. The ratios include a primary reserve ratio, which measures ability of the college to meet its debt obligation with readily available assets; a net operating revenue ratio, which indicates whether the institution ends the year with a surplus or a deficit; a return on net assets ratio, which measures whether the institution is better off financially than in prior years as indicated by net assets; a viability ratio, which measures whether the institution has available assets to cover debt should the institution need to settle obligations as of the balance sheet date; and an equity ratio, a ratio of financial assets to physical assets which measures an institution's flexibility in meeting financial needs (KPMG, 1999; Salluzzo, Prager, Mezzina, Cowen, & Tahey, 2010).

Some states set administrative rules for the fiscal management of colleges. Examples include the *Fiscal Management Manual* of the Illinois Community College Board (ICCB, 2014) and the Texas Higher Education Coordinating Board's *Budget Requirements and Annual Financial Reporting Requirements for Texas Public Community and Junior Colleges* (THECB, 2013a). Even with rules, colleges may have latitude to determine a number of fiscal management policies and practices within the state rules and regulations.

The prescriptiveness of state requirements varies. For example, some states have policies or procedures affecting institutions' reserve funds. Minnesota State Colleges and Universities (MNSCU) system, for example, requires institutions that have a general fund reserve below 5% to report on their fiscal condition with a plan to achieve this minimum reserve level. Any MNSCU institutions that wish to retain a reserve above 7% must have a plan approved by the system chief financial officer (MNSCU, 2014). In contrast, Illinois community colleges may retain whatever reserves they accumulate without seeking Illinois Community College Board approval.

Another key way in which state requirements affect the finances of individual community colleges is through statewide personnel contracts that set salaries and benefits, obligating local institutions to adhere to contractual agreements. For example, Massachusetts has a statewide faculty/professional staff contract, negotiated with a union (the Massachusetts Community College Council), that sets salaries for those teaching credit courses in the continuing education programs of the state's community colleges regardless of whether they are located in high-cost metropolitan centers such as Boston or rural communities such as Greenfield (Massachusetts Board of Higher Education, n.d.).

The key point here is to be aware that state legislation, policies, rules, and procedures may have profound impacts on community college budgets and finance, often limiting the freedom and flexibility with which institutions can make decisions perceived to be in their best interests.

Measures of Fiscal Accountability of Community Colleges

The simplest form of assessing financial health in a community college is to determine whether revenues exceed or are equal to expenditures. This is the same as balancing a household checkbook—if the sum of the money spent exceeds the sum of deposits, then the household is in financial jeopardy. Taking this one step further, a ratio analysis of various revenue streams against total expenditures can be used to gauge financial health. As Middaugh (2010) notes, "A college or university has certain fundamental revenue streams" and it also has fundamental expense categories, the sum of which "is referred to as 'total education and general expenditures'" (pp. 164–165). Revenue streams, Middaugh continues, derive from tuition and mandatory fees, contracts and grants, government appropriations, gifts, endowment and investment income, auxiliary operations (e.g., food service and bookstores), and other sources; expenditures include those related to instruction, extension and public service, academic support, student services, physical plant operations and maintenance, student aid, and departmental and sponsored research. Middaugh (2010) points out that "As important as it is to monitor revenue streams as broad gauges of institutional effectiveness, it is equally important to monitor how resources are being spent; this is usually referred to as an examination of expenditure demand." He goes on to say that, "Once again, ratio analysis is the analytical vehicle, with education and general expenditures continuing as the divisor" (pp. 167–168).

An example can be seen in the sophisticated set of financial indices and ratios created by the THECB (2013a, 2013b) to measure the financial health of the state's community colleges. Similar to the ratios required by the HLC, these measures have fairly universal currency. The state's General Appropriates Act requires annual reports to identify colleges that may be facing financial stress. In addition to using ratios encompassed in a Composite Financial Index (CFI), a composite of four metrics (the primary reserve ratio, viability ratio, return on net assets, and operating margin [surplus or deficit in fiscal year]), Texas also examines the equity leverage ratios, the latter a measure of the amount of debt in relation to net assets, which "provides an indication of the amount of debt service the institution must absorb into the future relative to existing resources" (THECB, 2013b, p. 5). The Board has established thresholds for quantitative indicators that suggest an institution could face financial stress (THECB, 2013b).

One area calling for special attention is deferred maintenance. As Middaugh (2010) notes, the "higher the proportion of deferred maintenance, the greater the potential drain on institutional resources" (p. 163). Accordingly, highly effective colleges allocate "two percent of the replacement value of the physical plant for facilities renewal and renovation" (p. 163). Another way to assess the cost of deferred maintenance is through the facilities condition index (FCI), defined as "the total estimated cost to complete deferred maintenance projects for the building by its estimated replacement value. The lower the FCI, the lower the need for remedial or renewal funding relative to the facility's value" (Soni, 2012, para. 2). The FCI can help an institution assess the cost of deferred maintenance for specific buildings on campus, though the political costs and benefits of demolition versus new construction will not be reflected in this quantitative indicator. By "political costs," we mean "costs" such as alienating a community that has great affection for a building, believing it has historical or architectural merit, or expanding the footprint of building onto land that had been devoted to a park. Addressing deferred maintenance is also likely to be a first casualty when unexpected financial challenges confront an institution, as a college is likely to use funds to preserve instructional programs and essential services rather than to fix old heating or ventilating systems that still creak along.

Fiscal Policies and Procedures

In addition to the development of the fiscal indicators, measuring fiscal health in community colleges requires an assessment of the college's financial policies and procedures. At a very basic level, these policies should emphasize adherence to generally accepted accounting principles and practices, such as those of the National Association of College and University Business Officers (n.d.). For example, public colleges and universities are required to use a fund accounting system; in this system, commingling of funds is not permitted and money in each fund must be used for the purposes of that fund. Funds are self-balancing sets of accounts for recording assets, liabilities, a fund balance, and changes in the fund balance. Funds are organized according to the activities and objectives specified by the college's governing board. Here is an example of the primary funds from a public community college (Oakton Community College, 2011):

- *Education fund* to support the fundamental education and support services of the college.
- *Operations and maintenance fund* to support operation and maintenance of the buildings and property, utilities costs, and staff.
- *Auxiliary enterprises fund* for services where a fee is charged to students/staff; examples include food service, the bookstore, and intercollegiate athletics.
- *Audit fund* to support required financial audits.
- *Liability, protection, and settlement fund* to provide for the payment of tort liability, property, and unemployment or worker's compensation insurance or claims.
- *Bond and interest fund* to hold revenues and pay expenses associated with outstanding bonds.

- *Educational foundation fund* to record financials of the college's educational foundation, a legally separate tax-exempt component unit of the institution.

These, of course, are not the only funds a community college might have. But regardless of the number of funds established, their use is essential to documenting how funds are spent. It may be helpful to think of each fund as a cookie jar with its own flavor of cookie. You can put chocolate chip cookies into its jar and remove chocolate chip cookies from it, but you cannot put oatmeal cookies into or take them from the chocolate chip cookie jar. The oatmeal cookies require a jar of their own.

Economic Evaluation

Economic evaluations are also valuable tools for assessing community college finances. McDavid and Hawthorn (2006) describe three types of analysis that might be undertaken. Note that they use the term "economic evaluation," but one might just as easily substitute "financial evaluation" or "fiscal evaluation." McDavid and Hawthorn focus more on programs and services than on the institution as a whole. One type of analysis is *cost–benefit analysis* in which costs and outcomes of a program or initiative are monetized (i.e., converted to dollar values) and compared to revenues. For example, a college might compare the money spent on student recruitment with the revenue generated by new students. *Cost-effectiveness analysis* is a second approach. Here, costs are compared to a single outcome that can be stated quantitatively, such as the number or percent of students who persist to the next term, and the third approach is *cost–utility analysis* wherein costs are compared to several outcomes that have been combined into one measurement unit, such as "student success" (defined as a combination of term-to-term persistence, successful course completions, and certificates or degrees awarded). Choosing which method to use depends on how challenging it is to monetize benefits, whether there is one or more than one outcome, and finally, what is required for the situation. For example, if two program alternatives are intended to produce the same outcome (e.g., helping students complete their degrees and certificates), then a cost-effectiveness analysis could determine which alternative delivers more graduates for the same cost.

Another approach to economic evaluation focuses on resource management. As Saunders (2001) notes:

> Resource management is a concept used in business and economic analysis to analyze the resources required to produce a unit of output. Applying this definition to higher education, or other non-profit organizations is difficult because of lack of agreement about what the "output" is in higher education. In higher education, is the output students? Research advancement? New and

improved medical knowledge? A better community? Recreation? Job training? Literacy training? Specific skill training for business? The answer is all of these and perhaps more. (p. 107)

Resource allocation and management studies are laden with both conceptual and methodological issues. For example, how are costs of education and services determined, and do they include both direct and indirect costs? How are prices set, and who makes these decisions? How are efficiency and productivity defined and measured? Can comparisons across institutions be made when colleges may calculate and allocate costs and revenues differently? How do institutions account for faculty and staff compensation derived through grants rather than through institutional resources? Are technology costs assigned to users or budgeted centrally? What programs and services are classified as auxiliary enterprises, and do auxiliary service revenues fund other activities or programs at the college?

Indicators of Community College Finances

In addition to the four economic evaluation approaches mentioned previously, and the financial ratios discussed earlier with respect to the HLC and the Texas Higher Education Coordinating Board, we examine three indicators of community college finances: productivity, economic impact studies, and bond ratings.

Productivity. In terms of productivity, the University of Delaware, working with peer institutions, in 1992 began a study of instructional costs and productivity that has grown over the years and is now known as the National Study of Instructional Costs & Productivity (see www.udel.edu/IR/cost/). As noted on the study's website:

> The National Study of Instructional Costs & Productivity, better known to many of you as the Delaware Cost Study, is generally acknowledged as the "tool of choice" for comparative analysis of faculty teaching loads, direct instructional cost, and separately budgeted scholarly activity, at the level of the academic discipline. (University of Delaware, 2011, para. 1)

The annual study collects information at the department or discipline level on teaching loads, faculty types, direct instructional costs, and indirect costs (Middaugh & Isaacs, 2003).

Some 10 years later, the National Community College Cost & Productivity Project (NCCCPP), originally known as the Kansas Study, was launched (see www.ncccpp.org). Modeled after the Delaware Study, the NCCCPP provides benchmarks at the discipline level for instructional costs per student credit hour; student–faculty ratios; workload by full-time, part-time, and other faculty; and students taught by full-time, part-time, and other faculty. Participating institutions are able to compare themselves with other NCCCPP colleges. More than 200 institutions have participated in the study since its inception. A key premise underlying both studies is that departments have control, at least to some extent, over departmental budgets and teaching loads and can, therefore, influence instructional costs and productivity at the departmental or discipline level.

However, the reality of community college governance makes it difficult if not impossible to do this. Most community colleges operate within systems and labor agreements that provide little opportunity for using differential salaries or teaching loads to attract, retain, and reward individual faculty members or faculty in hard-to-find disciplines. In many community colleges, full-time faculty teach significant amounts of overload, making it difficult to determine whether the proportion of courses or credits taught by full-time compared to part-time faculty is based on full-time faculty base loads or the combination of base and overload. Additionally, many community college budgets centralize accounts for equipment, tutors, and support staff rather than allocating these to departments. Thus, the ability of individual departments or disciplines to affect their costs is limited at best, and although comparing departmental costs and productivity across institutions can be interesting, it remains to be seen whether the data can actually be useful in driving decisions that affect departments.

Economic Impact Studies.   Economic impact studies comprise a different set of indicators to evaluate the economics of a community college (EMSI, 2014). Such studies attempt to determine the impact a college has on its local community, region, or state by examining both direct and indirect spending attributable to the college. Direct expenditures include salaries, purchases of goods and services, and capital construction. Economic impact studies use various multiplier calculations, which measure the spending stimulated by the direct expenditures. For example, a college faculty member will spend money at local restaurants and drycleaners, and these businesses will in turn hire employees and buy goods and services. It is often difficult if not impossible for community college students and employees to report how much money they spend in the college's official service area, especially in suburban communities where employees and to some extent students live across a wider geographical area than the college's district. Economic impact studies have grown more sophisticated over the years and now often include analyses such as increased earnings of community college graduates; at the same time, there is growing recognition of the significant overlap between colleges and other businesses in terms of the total economic contributions generated (Christophersen, Nadreau, & Olanie, 2014). Many economic impact studies portray institutions as making substantial economic contributions to their local service areas, though "substantial" in this context lacks a specific metric. Useful for public relations purposes, it is unclear whether such studies are useful approaches to actually evaluating the fiscal benefits and effectiveness of a college.

NEW DIRECTIONS FOR COMMUNITY COLLEGES • DOI: 10.1002/cc

Bond Ratings.   Finally, bond ratings are a third indicator of the economics of a community college. Moody's uses a multidimensional approach for rating general obligation bonds issued by U.S. local governments, including community colleges. Using four broad ratings factors—economic strength, financial strength, management and governance, and debt profile—Moody's rates the creditworthiness of an institution (Moody's Investors Service, 2009). The higher the rating, the lower the interest the institution will have to pay on its bonds, though the interest rate is also affected by interest rates across the economy at the time the bonds are actually issued. Colleges take pride in earning high Moody's ratings not just because the cost of borrowing will be less, but because a strong rating is often perceived as an indicator of financial health and good management.

Other Approaches to Examining Financial Health

Dickmeyer (2013) suggests a number of cost reports that could support decision making in key college areas. Though cautioning against specific "roadblocks" to the calculation and reporting of cost data, he posits that accurate cost data would help a college evaluate the change efforts incorporated in its strategic plan and focus efforts to achieve the desired outcomes. He provides examples related to assessing the payoff for investing in various change efforts: student success initiatives, establishing tuition amounts, and investment opportunities. Manning and Crosta, in Chapter 4 of this volume, as well as Romano, Losinger, and Millard (2011), offer examples of how cost analyses can lead to insights about program costs, both in terms of the costs implied in officially published program requirements and the costs of the varying pathways that students actually take as they pursue various credentials. Tracking these costs over time would allow a college to determine if its course and degree offerings make fiscal sense or whether resources are more effectively allocated to different offerings.

In addition, assessments of the fiscal health of community colleges should involve examinations of the financial effectiveness of external grants and philanthropic donations. Although the first review of these external funds should be an examination of the total revenue they generate, many subsequent questions arise. Are grant-funded employees covered by the same policies and procedures as employees funded through the college's regular budget? Are there provisions or obligations for retaining employees if the grant expires or is terminated? Is there any internal incentive, such as retention of indirect costs, to encourage departments to apply for external grants? Are there criteria for determining whether or not to seek external grants? With respect to philanthropy, does the institution have a foundation? To what extent are foundation policies and practices aligned with institutional policies and goals? Who makes decisions about whether the foundation will or should support specific projects and activities?

Drummer and Marshburn discuss philanthropy and external foundation grants in more detail in Chapter 7.

Conclusion

It seems as if it would be simple to document an institution's costs and revenues, to calculate the net revenues or losses for the institution and units within it, and to identify indicators that internal managers and external agencies can both understand and use to assess the financial health of an institution and its effectiveness in using resources to achieve its goals and objectives. But this is a dream. Although assessing an institution's health may be straightforward in the abstract, it is more complicated in practice. As this chapter indicates, there are not only many approaches to and indicators for evaluating the finances of a community college, there are also conceptual and technical issues in using each one.

Regardless of the approach used, here are some general guidelines that will be helpful to those responsible for assessing community college finances:

- Understand and review financial ratios used by state systems and accreditors, but don't assume that positive metrics mean the college is effectively using its funds to achieve desired outcomes, or that negative ratios spell trouble. For example, Austin Community College in Texas has incurred debt to support its planned expansion, but most of the debt is supported by taxes dedicated to that purpose; the tax rate is whatever is needed to service the debt. However, financial ratios do not include the guaranteed tax revenue, and the college appears on paper to be exceeding an appropriate debt level (B. Ferrell, personal communication, March 3, 2014).
- Remember that those who assess the fiscal health and financial effectiveness of a community college often have conflicting interpretations about what makes a college financially "healthy" and "effective." Ben Ferrell, executive vice president of finance and administration at Austin Community College, provides an example. He notes that bond raters such as Moody's like large reserves because they perceive this as protecting bondholders, whereas local taxpayers and students may wonder why an institution raises its tax rate or increases tuition when it has what they perceive to be a great deal of money in the bank (B. Ferrell, personal communication, March 3, 2014).
- Money cannot measure everything and may not even measure what is important beyond basic financial solvency. Fiscal calculations cannot capture the extent to which students feel engaged in and welcomed by their colleges, faculty create learning environments that promote student interest in the topic and academic success, students acquire the knowledge and skills expected of graduates in their programs, employees like coming to work, and the community feels a sense of pride in its local

college. Some of the poorest colleges economically have faculty and staff who take enormous pride in their institutions and genuinely like being there, whereas other institutions with strong financial bases have dissatisfied faculty and staff who concentrate on the negative. Similarly, some of the poorest colleges score higher on student success measures than their wealthier counterparts.

- There is no single metric to measure financial health or effectiveness other than, perhaps, a bottom line indicating the college has spent virtually all funds, including its reserve and endowments, and cannot even meet payroll. Identifying and reporting multiple measures are essential.
- Most community college leaders, and certainly faculty, are less interested in the finances of a college than in their own teaching and their students' learning. Boards, presidents, and other top leaders need to mind the financial store on behalf of their communities, employees, and students.

References

Christophersen, K., Nadreau, T., & Olanie, A. (2014, January 7). *The rights and wrongs of economic impact analysis for colleges and universities*. Retrieved from EMSI website: http://www.economicmodeling.com/2014/01/07/the-rights-and-wrongs-of-economic-impact-analysis-for-colleges-and-universities/

Dickmeyer, N. (2013, June). Time for a reporting do-over. *Business Officer Magazine*. Retrieved from http://www.nacubo.org/Business_Officer_Magazine/Magazine_Archives/June_2013/

EMSI. (2014, February). *Where value meets values: The economic impact of community colleges*. Retrieved from http://www.aacc.nche.edu/About/Documents/USA_AGG_MainReport_Final_021114.pdf

Ewell, P. T. (2011). Accountability and institutional effectiveness in the community college. In R. B. Head (Ed.), *New Directions for Community Colleges: No. 53. Institutional effectiveness* (pp. 23–36). San Francisco, CA: Jossey-Bass.

Head, R. B. (2011). The evolution of institutional effectiveness in the community college. In R. B. Head (Ed.), *New Directions for Community Colleges: No. 53. Institutional effectiveness* (pp. 5–11). San Francisco, CA: Jossey-Bass.

Head, R. B., & Johnson, M. S. (2011). Accreditation and its influence on institutional effectiveness. In R. B. Head (Ed.), *New Directions for Community Colleges: No. 53. Institutional effectiveness* (pp. 37–52). San Francisco, CA: Jossey-Bass.

Higher Learning Commission. (2013). *The criteria for accreditation*. Retrieved from http://policy.ncahlc.org/Policies/criteria-for-accreditation.html

Illinois Community College Board (ICCB). (2014). *Fiscal management manual*. Retrieved from http://www.iccb.state.il.us/pdf/fiscal_manuals/FMM14.pdf

KPMG. (1999). *Ratio analysis in higher education: Measuring past performance to chart future directions* (4th ed.). New York, NY: KPMG LLP and Prager, McCarthy & Sealy, LLC.

Massachusetts Board of Higher Education. (n.d.). *Agreement for division of continuing education*. Retrieved from http://mccc-union.org/CONTRACTS/DCE%202009-2012/DCE%20Contract%202009-2012.pdf

McDavid, J. C., & Hawthorn, L. R. L. (2006). *Program evaluation & performance measurement: An introduction to practice*. Thousand Oaks, CA: Sage.

Middaugh, M. F. (2010). *Planning and assessment in higher education*. San Francisco, CA: Jossey-Bass.

Middaugh, M. F., & Isaacs, H. K. (2003). Describing faculty activity and productivity for multiple audiences. In W. E. Knight (Ed.), *The primer for institutional research* (pp. 24–46). Tallahassee, FL: Association for Institutional Research.

Minnesota State Colleges and Universities (MNSCU). (2014). *Procedure 5.10.1 general operating fund reserve.* Retrieved from http://www.mnscu.edu/board/procedure/510p1.html

Moody's Investors Service. (2009, October). *Rating methodology: General obligation bonds issued by U.S. local governments.* Retrieved from http://wauwatosa.net/DocumentCenter/View/2197

National Association of College and University Business Officers. (n.d.). *Accounting standards.* Retrieved from http://www.nacubo.org/Business_and_Policy_Areas/Accounting/Accounting_Standards.html

Oakton Community College. (2011). *Presentation budget 2011–2012.* Retrieved from http://www.oakton.edu/about/officesanddepartments/financial_services/annual_budgets/annualbudgetFY2012.pdf

Romano, R. M., Losinger, R., & Millard, T. (2011). Measuring the cost of a degree: A case study of a SUNY community college. *Community College Review, 39,* 211–234.

Salluzzo, R. E., Prager, F. J., Mezzina, L., Cowen, C. J., & Tahey, P. (2010). *Strategic financial analysis for higher education* (7th ed.). New York, NY: Prager, Sealy & Co., LLC; KPMG, LLP; Attain, LLC.

Saunders, L. (2001). Resource management and quality improvement. In R. D. Howard (Ed.), *Institutional research: Decision support in higher education* (pp. 107–130). Tallahassee, FL: Association for Institutional Research.

Soni, A. (2012). *What is the facilities condition index?* Retrieved from http://www.vfa.com/2012/03/what-is-the-facility-condition-index/

Southern Association of Colleges and Schools Commission on Colleges (SACSCOC). (2012). *The principles of accreditation: Foundations of quality enhancement* (5th ed.). Decatur, GA: Author.

Texas Higher Education Coordinating Board (THECB). (2013a). *Budget requirements and annual financial reporting requirements for Texas public community and junior colleges, FY 2013.* Retrieved from http://www.thecb.state.tx.us/reports/PDF/3069.PDF

Texas Higher Education Coordinating Board (THECB). (2013b). *Financial condition analysis of the Texas public community college districts, 2013.* Retrieved from http://www.thecb.state.tx.us/reports/PDF/3055.PDF

University of Delaware. (2011, May). *The national study of instructional costs & productivity.* Newark, DE: Author. Retrieved from www.udel.edu/IR/cost/

Trudy H. Bers is the president of the Bers Group, an educational consulting company, and an adjunct professor at the University of Maryland University College, Adelphi, MD.

Ronald B. Head is a professor and an assistant chair of the Doctor of Management Program in Community College Leadership and Policy at the University of Maryland University College, Adelphi, MD.

New Directions for Community Colleges • DOI: 10.1002/cc

10

Besides the shift in community college funding from the state to the student, a number of other innovations and trends have emerged with respect to community college finances. This chapter explores some of these developments, including performance-based funding, changes in student and institutional eligibility for financial aid, changes in local funding, generating revenue from institutional data, and the potential financial impact of massive open online courses (MOOCs). Clearly, the financial landscape of community colleges is changing dramatically, calling for more skillful financial managers and entrepreneurs.

Evolving Practices and Emerging Innovations in Community College Finance

Christopher M. Mullin

While the Great Recession technically ended in 2009, it continues to hold sway on the financing of community colleges in 2014. This constrained fiscal environment, coupled with the immediacy of pressures from external sources for greater attention to student success and internal pressures on institutional operations, necessitates new ways of thinking about sources of revenue for community colleges.

Historically, community colleges have relied heavily on funding for student participation in the form of state appropriations based on enrollment and gross tuition and fee revenue (inclusive of student financial aid). In approximately 25 states (Palmer, 2008), community colleges receive local property tax funding in addition to state tax appropriations. Today, traditional funding approaches are changing, new policies affecting financial aid are having profound effects on both student enrollment and college revenues, and technology advances and new instructional delivery modes are shifting college finances. It is this evolution of existing practices in traditional funding sources that may have the most direct and near-term influence on community college finance.

NEW DIRECTIONS FOR COMMUNITY COLLEGES, no. 168, Winter 2014 © 2014 Wiley Periodicals, Inc.
Published online in Wiley Online Library (wileyonlinelibrary.com) • DOI: 10.1002/cc.20125

The evolution of existing practices in the funding of community colleges, as well as the apparent cost shifting from public subsidies to students, provides today's impetus for seeking new sources of revenue as a way of maintaining affordable open access to educational opportunity. Emerging innovations have the potential to provide stable revenues for community colleges. The benefit of these new revenue sources is that they are not treated as policy levers by external agencies seeking to exert control over institutional actions. This provides institutions with flexibility in raising and using funds to meet their unique missions.

The purpose of this chapter is to examine both evolving practices and emerging innovations in greater detail, with a focus on examples of current practice and potential opportunities for action.

Evolving Practices

Calls for greater institutional efficiency and productivity traditionally follow economic downturns. However, efficiency and productivity are not new ideas in higher education. What is new is the increasing influence of state and federal government goals on the allocation of state funds and federal student aid. New developments related to performance funding, student aid, and local funding reflect this shift.

Performance Funding.   Paying for performance is one way of tying the funding of colleges with the outcomes desired—even expected—by state governments. Performance funding, which ties an institution's allocation to such outcome indicators as completions and success rates (i.e., completion plus transfer), first emerged in Tennessee in 1979 and has been instituted in various forms in other states since that time. The first wave of performance funding (often called *performance funding 1.0*) came in the 1990s and was studied largely by Joseph Burke and colleagues at the State University of New York's Rockefeller Institute of Government (www.rockinst.org/education/accountability_higher_ed.aspx). This research provided a greater understanding of what performance funding was and how it was being operationalized by states. In 2003, Burke and Minassians noted the shift away from performance funding to the less costly and less controversial option of performance reporting (where funds were not linked to performance). Shulock (2011) identified four shortcomings of performance funding 1.0 models: the limited amount (2% or less) of funding that was allocated by performance funding models; the overemphasis on metrics that did not reflect the community college mission; the incorporation of unreasonable targets, which made success difficult to obtain; and the designation of most performance funding dollars as categorical funding allocated in addition to, rather than embedded in, traditional funding streams, which made them ripe for defunding.

Currently, colleges are being affected by the second era of performance funding, which has been called *performance funding 2.0*. This iteration seeks to differentiate itself from its predecessors by connecting colleges to the needs of the state and students rather than focusing on the fiscal needs of institutions themselves (McKweon-Moak & Mullin, 2014).

The research on performance funding is both limited and mixed (Burke, 2002; Dougherty & Reddy, 2011), with little known about its true impact on students and states. Mullin, Baime, and Honeyman (in press) suggest that a causal impact may never be identified because so many other factors and programs confound any analysis, including the presence of other funding streams and related expectations, changes to student aid eligibility, changes in financial aid and in institutional funding schemes that are designed to incentivize student and college behaviors, and the presence of numerous federal, state, college, and nonprofit foundation efforts focused on student success. The primary benefit of performance funding is, at its core, its role as a policy tool that allows external stakeholders to exercise some level of control or influence over institutional operations.

Student Aid Eligibility Changes.   The criteria used to allocate need-based financial aid are of substantial importance to the funding of student populations who tend to enroll at community colleges. Any change to student or institutional eligibility criteria is therefore of the highest importance. Yet, ongoing changes in the eligibility criteria for both students and institutions continually build upon old ideas to create new ways of thinking.

By and large, community college students have benefited substantially from the Pell Grant program. Since the early 1990s, students attending community colleges have received nearly one third of all Pell Grant funds as compared to approximately one quarter of all Pell funds in the 1980s; at the same time, the number of community college students receiving a Pell Grant increased from 1 million in 1980–1981 to 2.6 million in 2010–2011 (Baime & Mullin, 2011). As tuition and fees become an ever-increasing source of college revenues, and as the related costs of attendance covered by the Pell Grant—such as books and supplies—increased, community college leaders have sought to ensure that alterations to student eligibility criteria do not remove from eligibility the types of students community colleges have traditionally served.

Many changes in Pell eligibility have been enacted and proposed over time (Cook & King, 2007; Mahan, 2011; Wolanin, 1998). Three enacted and two proposed changes that garnered substantial attention from federal policymakers have important consequences for community college students because they reflect conversations about not only who should benefit from college, but the expectation that students should exhibit college-going behaviors that decrease the time to a credential. The following paragraphs examine the estimated impacts of each, though not their combined effect.

Time Limits.   A recent evolution in student eligibility criteria for the Pell Grant program included limiting the amount of time a student could receive an award, based in part upon the idea that it would incentivize students to complete college in a more timely fashion. The Congressional

Budget Office (2011) suggested that reducing the number of years a student may receive a Pell Grant from 9 to 6 would save $5.6 billion in program costs and $5.1 billion in budgetary outlays over 10 years. But an analysis of data from the National Postsecondary Student Aid Study (NPSAS) for college students enrolled in 2008[1] suggests that reducing the number of years a student may receive the Pell Grant to 6 from 9 would eliminate from eligibility 1.8% of the student body at private, not-for-profit four-year institutions as compared to 0.8% of the student body at public two-year institutions. These data do not account for students who transfer, so it may be the case that four-year college students who initially started at public two-year institutions would be impacted by this change. This change went into effect with passage of the Consolidated Appropriations Act of 2012.

Ability to Benefit (ATB) Students.   In the wake of concerns that institutions were enrolling students who may not be able to benefit from college, tighter eligibility criteria for students deemed able to benefit from college were proposed. An analysis of NPSAS data for college students enrolled in 2008 suggests that for-profit institutions had the greatest percentage of their student body (2.6%) without a high school degree or certificate (a proxy for ability-to-benefit [ATB] status), with community colleges next (1.2% of their student body). Further analysis of the NPSAS data found that in 2007–2008, 14,073 of the 100,374 ATB students at community colleges received Pell grants, suggesting that the change in eligibility criteria would affect approximately 14% of all ATB students at community colleges. This change also went into effect with passage of the Consolidated Appropriations Act of 2012.

Year-Round Pell Grant.   While students enroll in college at all times throughout the year, the Pell Grant is only available for a nine-month period of time. To assist students in a more timely completion of their credentials, the year-round Pell Grant (YRP) was put into place for the 2009–2010 academic year. But after one year of implementation, YRP was eliminated in part to maintain the maximum Pell Grant amount (Davidson, 2014). While still a concern among many community college leaders, unpublished data from the U.S. Department of Education suggest that community colleges were not the sector of higher education whose revenues were negatively impacted the most by the termination of the YRP; both public four-year and for-profit institutions received in excess of $500 million from YRP in 2009–2010, whereas community colleges did not.

Eliminating Less-Than-Half-Time Students.   Continuing an interest in incentivizing student behavior to complete a credential quickly, the Congressional Budget Office (2011) suggested that denying less-than-half-time students access to federal Pell grants would save $1.2 billion in program costs and $1.1 billion in budgetary outlays over 10 years. Analysis of data from the Office of Postsecondary Education (2010)[1] suggested that approximately 54,000 of the Pell recipients enrolled less than half time attend public two-year colleges and would be subject to losing awards. A total of just over

Figure 10.1. Tuition, Fees, Books, and Supplies Relative to the Pell Grant Maximum Amount, 2011–2012

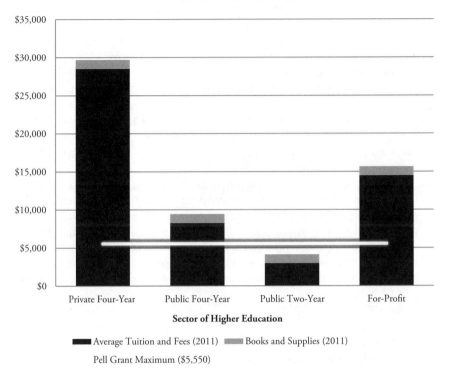

Sector of Higher Education

■ Average Tuition and Fees (2011) ▬ Books and Supplies (2011)
Pell Grant Maximum ($5,550)

108,000 Pell recipients were enrolled less than half time in 2009–2010. This proposed change had not been enacted at the time this chapter was written.

Disallowing Room and Board for Students in Distance Education. The proposed elimination of all expenses except those for tuition, fees, books, and supplies will have a negative impact only on students attending community colleges, because only in the case of community colleges does the maximum Pell Grant award exceed the price of tuition, fees, books, and supplies, resulting in the inability of these students to receive the maximum award amount. In other sectors of higher education, students pay a higher price and would therefore be eligible to receive the entire Pell Grant maximum award (see Figure 10.1). The proposed elimination was estimated to place an extra financial burden of nearly $1,400 on distance education students at community colleges. This proposed change had not been enacted at the time this chapter was written.

Institutional Eligibility. Institutions also have to meet a set of conditions to be eligible to participate in federal student aid programs, including Pell. Requirements, conditions, and situations where waivers may be granted are detailed in Part 600 of the Code of Federal Regulations (2013).

Changes being considered at the time this chapter was written relate to adding performance thresholds on institutionally based metrics dealing with access, affordability, and outcomes to institutional eligibility requirements for participating in federal student aid programs such as the Pell Grant. At present, the metrics under consideration, which may be applied to either an institution or a program at an institution, are being developed as part of the Postsecondary Institution Rating System (PIRS). The intent is to publish them before the 2015 academic year (U.S. Department of Education, n.d.).

Local Funding.   Long a hallmark of the local nature of community colleges, local funding for colleges has become challenging in many states as property values fluctuate in response to economic conditions. In the 25 states in which community colleges receive more than 10% of revenues from local sources, the local role in funding is not new. What is new is an attempt to add local funding in other states. Florida, for example, introduced legislation (HB 113) in 2014 to allow for local funding in the form of a half-penny sales tax to support community colleges and universities should these institutions exist in a particular county. While the legislation was ultimately unsuccessful, the effort by Miami-Dade College—which has long been a bellwether institution—to implement such a policy may serve as the foundation for further action.

Emerging Innovations

A lesson of the recent Great Recession for many was the need for institutions to diversify their revenue sources. Common yet still appropriate responses include focusing on fundraising efforts and contract training to identify additional revenue for colleges. This section explores those new sources of revenue that support unique institutional missions and examines the impact they may have on community college finances. The northern star for the emerging innovations to come is the recognition and potential power of technological advancements that are poised to provide new opportunities for financing. This section examines the opportunities these emerging innovations portend.

New Uses for Data.   A potential new source of revenue stems from expanding how the data an institution collects and maintains may be monetized. Namely, the data can be de-identified, aggregated, packaged, and sold. The possibilities for monetizing data have increased tremendously as computer technology becomes more fully integrated into instruction.

Methods of delivering education have never been confined to classrooms. Cooperative ventures, internships, placements, fieldwork, semesters abroad, and work-based learning comprise a list of delivery methods occurring outside of an institution's walls. In addition, distance learning has a long history, going back to correspondence study via the mail and evolving over time as communication technologies (e.g., radio, television, and satellite feed) emerged. What is unique about the current evolution of instruction is how advancements in computer-based technology attempt to merge broad access and a personalized experience, thereby flipping the paradigm from students going out into the world to gain experience to bringing certain experiences around the world to the student. Simulators, for example, have been used to assist future pilots, and this technology can be extended to virtual tours of international locations. Students and student teachers can now virtually "experience" a classroom using avatar-like students who present challenges allowing aspiring teachers to hone their craft before they ever enter the classroom.

This evolution suggests that all classrooms will become virtual, even the ones that meet within the brick and mortar of a traditional classroom space at "traditional" times. In fact, the way we interact within the classroom environment is increasingly becoming digitized; indeed, this is already happening, as clickers provide instantaneous feedback, homework gets submitted electronically, and voice recognition software captures ideas. Furthermore, we are quickly moving to a time when the institutional functions of classrooms, registrars, student affairs, and student aid are no longer separate but, rather, combined in an information technology infrastructure that transforms the student user interface into a seamless experience while providing administrators a holistic look at a student's collegiate experience.

Advancements in technology allow each interaction, from each person, to be accounted for, tracked, and combined in unprecedented ways. It is all of the data people submit without fully thinking about it—such as web pages visited, links clicked, times of day connecting, or length of visit—that allows for a more customizable user experience. The term *data* has taken on a whole new meaning. No longer are data just the information that has to be disclosed or reported in aggregate about a cohort of students by an institutional research office as part of a historical record; rather data have become a source of information on the interactions individuals have with a college.

All students, faculty and staff members, members of the campus leadership, and innumerable alumni interact with colleges in their own ways, either directly through institutional technologies or indirectly through personal accounts on social media platforms such as Facebook or LinkedIn. These data can be linked with information available openly on the internet to build a massive file about each student, faculty member, staff member, leader, or alumnus. This new conception of what data are opens up conversations of how they are collected, what to do with them, and—of central importance to this discussion—how to monetize them.

Asking questions on student surveys is a keystone of this approach. As an example, some student surveys ask students how they identify themselves in terms of political affiliation as part of a section focused on civic engagement. Aside from informing the college about the student body's level of civic engagement, these data could then be aggregated and sold to political parties, as an example, to assist them in better understanding the student demographic. The response-rate limitation could be overcome by requiring the survey for graduation, as is done at some colleges, or even upon enrollment.

Colleges sit on a wealth of data that they often do not monopolize and that they give away by not carefully examining contracts with vendors and service providers. If each contract was viewed in terms of the data that were being given away by college, it might be possible to renegotiate terms and either reduce the costs or find ways to capture lost revenue. For example, rather than giving an institution's data to a nonprofit organization that then sells it, it may be an option to charge the nonprofit organization for the data in addition to securing access to the data that the organization itself has collected from other colleges. One's imagination is the only limitation to finding ways of monetizing the wealth of data that colleges now collect. However, any use of data about individuals would, without question, need to be de-identified and aggregated to conform with provisions of the Family Educational Rights and Privacy Act (1974, 2013), any other relevant law or regulation, and best practices in data privacy and protection as provided by the U.S. Department of Education's Privacy Technical Assistance Center (2014).

The Fiscal Impact of MOOCs. Massive open online courses (MOOCs) have the potential to have both positive and negative fiscal impacts on community colleges. However, the conditions under which revenues increase more than they decrease remain unknown. At present, there exists great promise in the application of technology to remediate time and place barriers to learning. The fervor over asynchronous learning opportunities, on a broad scale beyond the boundaries of class size limits, offers potentially profound fiscal impacts—assuming the successful development and deployment of MOOCs.

A Limited Revenue Opportunity. Few colleges, and even fewer community colleges, can create a quality MOOC at all, let alone maintain them. So, the idea that MOOCs will result in a financial windfall for all colleges that wish to offer them is false. The promise of MOOCs clearly lies with well-financed institutions or third-party entities that have the required infrastructure, expertise, and capital. Less resourced colleges could purchase the courses and then charge students a convenience fee or tuition and fees for supplementary instruction. In either model, the financial costs of production will eventually be pushed onto the user—the student. Costs may be reduced by advertisements and product placement within the learning platform, as is common for many mobile apps. There are undoubtedly numerous other ways to commercialize learning opportunities.

MOOCs may be a fad, and their future in community college finance may be overstated. A more strategic approach may be to ensure that any and all data collected in any platform be retained, "owned," and monetized by the college rather than the provider—or to at least establish boundaries of use in MOOC contracts, with substantial penalties for those who violate use policies.

The End of the Autonomous Small College. It may be argued that MOOCs, if widespread, will result in a substantial transfer of institutional revenues from smaller, less resourced institutions to larger, well-resourced institutions. Institutions that plan to heavily depend upon externally developed MOOCs may also become educational intermediaries—branch campuses of a centralized organization. In doing so, MOOCs may well threaten the historically market-informed differentiation of institutions. Taken to the extreme, MOOCs weaken the structure and value of institutional autonomy and intellectual diversity. The centralization, and concomitantly the standardization, of information development, distribution, and evaluation in an outcome-focused environment may be seen by some—especially researchers seeking to determine some type of impact—as a very good thing.

Should MOOCs take hold in this way, increases in scale and costs may eradicate small colleges as they exist today. Furthermore, as is the case in some for-profit colleges currently, Tayloresque operations of job functions may well dismantle the teaching craft into its scientific parts—lecturer, test developer, advisor, knowledge expert, and so on. Although the end of craftsmanship, as examined by Crawford (2009), is beyond the scope of this chapter, it is important to understand the potential future for college operations and funding.

What I have shared in this examination of MOOCs may well be controversial and I acknowledge that the future of MOOCs has yet to be determined. MOOCs may become nothing more than a correspondence course or a modern source of supplementary teaching materials relegated to the few and external to the core operations—and financing—of community colleges. Or they may not.

Moving Forward

Although community colleges are enjoying the spotlight during the Obama administration, the producers of the show still have no clue as to the nature of the talent on the stage. This is the guiding problem with community college finance today—there exists a desire for traditional outcomes in an era of nontraditional revenue sources.

This chapter began with a discussion of the evolutions that have occurred in traditional revenue streams to community colleges and closed with a discussion of emerging opportunities for identifying and securing new revenue sources. While the future is uncertain, the ongoing changes to funding examined in this chapter will continue forward; the only question is in what ways.

Note

1. The analysis was conducted by the author of this chapter. Tables are available upon request.

References

Baime, D. S., & Mullin, C. M. (2011, July). *Promoting educational opportunity: The Pell Grant program at community colleges* (Policy Brief 2011-03PBL). Washington, DC: American Association of Community Colleges.

Burke, J. C. (Ed.). (2002). *Funding public colleges and universities for performance: Popularity, problems, and prospects.* Albany, NY: Rockefeller Institute.

Burke, J., & Minassians, H. (2003). *Real accountability or accountability "lite": Seventh annual survey, 2003.* Albany, NY: Rockefeller Institute of Government.

Congressional Budget Office. (2011, March). *Reducing the deficit: Spending and revenue options.* Washington, DC: Author.

Consolidated Appropriations Act of 2012, H.R. 3671, 112th Cong. (2012). Retrieved from the U. S. Government Printing Office website: http://www.gpo.gov/fdsys/pkg/BILLS-112hr3671ih/pdf/BILLS-112hr3671ih.pdf

Cook, B. J., & King, J. E. (2007, June). *2007 status report on the Pell Grant program.* Washington, DC: American Council on Education, Center for Policy Analysis.

Crawford, M. B. (2009). *Shop class as soulcraft: An inquiry into the value of work.* New York, NY: Penguin Press.

Davidson, C. (2014, January). Changes to the Federal Pell Grant program eligibility: The effect of policy and program changes on college students at public institutions in Kentucky. *Journal of Student Financial Aid, 43*(3), 111–131.

Dougherty, K., & Reddy, V. (2011). *The impacts of state performance funding systems on higher education institutions: Research literature review and policy recommendations* (CCRC Working Paper No. 37). New York, NY: Community College Research Center, Teachers College, Columbia University.

Family Educational Rights and Privacy Act (FERPA) of 1974, 20 U.S.C. § 1232g (1974).

Family Educational Rights and Privacy Act (FERPA), 34 Code of Federal Regulations § 99 (2013).

HB 113: Discretionary sales surtaxes. Florida House of Representatives. (2014). Retrieved from http://www.myfloridahouse.gov/Sections/Bills/billsdetail.aspx?BillId=51229

Institutional Eligibility Under the Higher Education Act of 1965, 34 Code of Federal Regulations § 600 (2013).

Mahan, S. M. (2011, January 10). *Federal Pell Grant program and the Higher Education Act: Background, recent changes, and current legislative issues* (Report No. R41437). Washington, DC: Congressional Research Service.

McKweon-Moak, M., & Mullin, C. M. (2014). *Higher education finance research: Policy, politics, and practice.* Charlotte, NC: Information Age Publishing.

Mullin, C. M., Baime, D. S., & Honeyman, D. S. (in press). *Community college finance: A guide for institutional leaders.* San Francisco, CA: Jossey-Bass.

Office of Postsecondary Education. (2010). *Pell end-of-year report 2008-09.* Washington, DC: U.S. Department of Education.

Palmer, J. C. (2008). *Grapevine compilation of state higher education tax appropriations data for fiscal year 2008.* Normal, IL: Center for the Study of Education Policy, Illinois State University.

Privacy Technical Assistance Center. (2014). *Student privacy 101: FERPA for parents and students.* Retrieved from U.S. Department of Education website: http://ptac.ed.gov/

Shulock, N. (2011, May). *Concerns about performance-based funding and ways that states are addressing concerns* (IHELP Brief). Sacramento: California State University Sacramento.

U.S. Department of Education. (n.d.). *College ratings and paying for performance.* Retrieved from http://www.ed.gov/college-affordability/college-ratings-and-paying-performance

Wolanin, T. R. (1998). Pell grants: A 25-year history. In L. E. Gladieux, B. Astor, and W. S. Swail (Eds.), *Memory, reason, imagination: A quarter century of Pell Grants* (pp. 13–31). Washington, DC: College Entrance Examination Board.

CHRISTOPHER M. MULLIN *is the assistant vice chancellor for Policy and Research at the State University System of Florida, Board of Governors.*

11

Community college leaders face several fundamental challenges as they work on sustaining the fiscal viability of their institutions. These include the need to anticipate the unintended consequences of performance-based funding, diversify revenue streams in ways that reduce fiscal dependence on tuition and state appropriations, control costs, and rethink the comprehensive, all-things-for-all-people mission.

Concluding Thoughts

James C. Palmer

Fiscal administration at community colleges requires a familiarity with and competency in the many management strategies mentioned in the preceding chapters, including budgeting, linking budgets to plans, costing out student pathways, and fundraising. It also requires, as the preceding chapters have noted, a thorough understanding of state funding mechanisms and government accounting guidelines, the fiscal mandates of accrediting bodies, and other features of the fiscal regulatory environment in which community colleges, as public institutions, operate. All reflect the resource management skills listed by the American Association of Community Colleges (2005) in its document on *Competencies for Community College Leaders*.

Yet the chapters in this monograph also point to larger challenges faced by community college leaders in a fiscal environment that, for at least 40 years, has been marked by unpredictable and attenuated state funding caused by severe ups and downs in the economy as well as the increased competition for scarce state dollars from K–12 education, corrections, healthcare, and other equally compelling social services (Palmer, 2013). One challenge lies in the need to anticipate and work against the unintended consequences of state efforts to tie funding to performance, a trend that—despite the checkered history of these performance-funding mechanisms—continues to hold great appeal to state policymakers who struggle with the tension between growing dissatisfaction with student completion rates on the one hand and limited state tax revenues on the other. As Dowd and Shieh note in this volume, community college leaders will need to be vigilant against institutional responses to these

NEW DIRECTIONS FOR COMMUNITY COLLEGES, no. 168, Winter 2014 © 2014 Wiley Periodicals, Inc.
Published online in Wiley Online Library (wileyonlinelibrary.com) • DOI: 10.1002/cc.20126

performance-based funding incentives (such as restrictions on late registration) that might work against low-income or minority students. A key component of fiscal leadership will entail purposeful efforts to ensure that the goal of increased efficiency—doing more with less—does not displace the goal of equal access and opportunity.

A second challenge deals with the difficulties of diversifying revenue streams through fundraising and entrepreneurial efforts that have the potential to reduce institutional dependence on state funding and tuition. The former remains as uncertain as ever, whereas increases in the latter are becoming politically unsustainable. As a consequence, pressures will increase on the colleges not only to step up fundraising efforts, but also to consider new revenue sources, as discussed by Mullin in this volume, and leverage resources that are potentially available through partnerships with businesses and other area entities, as discussed in the chapters by Phelan (who emphasizes the need for community colleges to become a "networked organization") and by Cejda and Jolley. Both suggest entrepreneurial work as a key contributor to fiscal viability, though small community colleges serving economically depressed rural areas may be less able to move in this direction than larger colleges serving urban or suburban districts with relatively well-heeled industries. The ability to draw on resources in the community depends, of course, on the existence of those community resources to begin with.

Even if entrepreneurial efforts succeed in reducing dependency on state funds and tuition, colleges will still face the challenge of reducing costs. Just as the goal of increasing the proportion of the population that has healthcare coverage will depend as much on containing healthcare costs as it will on subsidizing healthcare coverage itself, so too will the goal of increasing the educational attainment of the population depend as much on cost containment as it will on public subsidies. As Lombardi (1973) noted at the beginning of the era of attenuated state support that we are still experiencing today, recurrent fiscal downturns require college leaders to look "inward as well as outward" (p. 120), searching for internal fiscal efficiencies as well as advocating for additional tax support. Fiscal leadership will therefore entail experimentation with alternative approaches for helping students, perhaps using the pathway costing techniques described by Manning and Crosta in this volume to determine if new advising techniques, revised orientations, or other interventions yield more cost-efficient routes to transfer or credential completion. Cost analysis will increasingly become an important component of the ways colleges evaluate student services and instructional approaches.

But perhaps the most formidable challenge in fiscal management today lies in the need to more precisely define the community college mission, moving away from the all-things-to-all-people stance of the traditional comprehensive curriculum to a mission that more precisely states what the college does and for whom. This move away from an all-inclusive comprehensiveness, emphasized in the chapter by Phelan, will require colleges to specify which aspects of career and adult education they will be responsible for and which will be ceded to partnering organizations in the community. A more focused mission will also require decisions about which students will be given first priority in state-subsidized college programming, a form of rationing that has long been a response to finite state resources. For example, after the 1978 passage of Proposition 13, a statewide tax limitation measure, many California community college districts cut back on community service and noncredit programs, giving the degree-seeking students in vocational and transfer programs a higher funding priority (Cohen & Brawer, 1982). This was later embodied in California's Seymour-Campbell Student Success Act of 2012 (Section 5), which specified matriculation services for students, "with a priority toward serving students who enroll to earn degrees, career technical certificates, transfer preparation, or career advancement." The view of the community college as an agency that is akin to a public library or museum, used by individuals for idiosyncratic purposes outside of transfer or credential attainment (Adelman, 1992), may not be sustainable in today's fiscal environment.

Any fiscal or budgeting technique is only as useful as the leadership context in which it is employed. Those seeking to secure additional funding or carry out the difficult task of budgeting and allocating resources across college programs can draw on well-vetted strategies and techniques discussed in this monograph and in the literature on higher education finance. But, as always, success will depend on well-articulated answers to the fundamental questions of "Funding for what?" and "Budgeting for what?" Leadership efforts to answer these questions in meaningful ways constitute the first step toward sound fiscal management.

References

Adelman, C. (1992). *The way we are: The community college as American thermometer.* Washington, DC: U.S. Department of Education.

American Association of Community Colleges. (2005). *Competencies for community college leaders.* Retrieved from http://www.aacc.nche.edu/Resources/competencies /Documents/compentenciesforleaders.pdf

Cohen, A. M., & Brawer, F. B. (1982). *The American community college* (1st ed.). San Francisco, CA: Jossey-Bass.

Lombardi, J. (1973). Critical decade for community college financing. In J. Lombardi (Ed.), *New Directions for Community Colleges: No. 2. Meeting the financial crisis* (pp. 109–120). San Francisco, CA: Jossey-Bass.

Palmer, J. (2013). State fiscal support for community colleges. In J. S. Levin & S. Kater (Eds.), *Understanding community colleges* (pp. 171–183). New York, NY: Routledge.

Seymour-Campbell Student Success Act of 2012, Cal. Edc. Code § 624. Retrieved from http://leginfo.legislature.ca.gov/faces/billNavClient.xhtml?bill_id=201120120SB1456

JAMES C. PALMER is a professor in the Department of Educational Administration and Foundations at Illinois State University, Normal, IL.

INDEX

NEW DIRECTIONS FOR COMMUNITY COLLEGE
ORDER FORM SUBSCRIPTION AND SINGLE ISSUES

DISCOUNTED BACK ISSUES:

Use this form to receive 20% off all back issues of *New Directions for Community College*.
All single issues priced at **$23.20** (normally $29.00)

TITLE	ISSUE NO.	ISBN

Call 1-800-835-6770 or see mailing instructions below. When calling, mention the promotional code JBNND to receive your discount. For a complete list of issues, please visit www.josseybass.com/go/ndcc

SUBSCRIPTIONS: (1 YEAR, 4 ISSUES)

☐ New Order   ☐ Renewal

U.S.	☐ Individual: $89	☐ Institutional: $335
CANADA/MEXICO	☐ Individual: $89	☐ Institutional: $375
ALL OTHERS	☐ Individual: $113	☐ Institutional: $409

Call 1-800-835-6770 or see mailing and pricing instructions below.
Online subscriptions are available at www.onlinelibrary.wiley.com

ORDER TOTALS:

Issue / Subscription Amount: $ _____

Shipping Amount: $ _____
(for single issues only – subscription prices include shipping)

Total Amount: $ _____

SHIPPING CHARGES:	
First Item	$6.00
Each Add'l Item	$2.00

(No sales tax for U.S. subscriptions. Canadian residents, add GST for subscription orders. Individual rate subscriptions must be paid by personal check or credit card. Individual rate subscriptions may not be resold as library copies.)

BILLING & SHIPPING INFORMATION:

☐ **PAYMENT ENCLOSED:** *(U.S. check or money order only. All payments must be in U.S. dollars.)*

☐ **CREDIT CARD:**   ☐ VISA   ☐ MC   ☐ AMEX

Card number _____ Exp. Date _____

Card Holder Name _____ Card Issue # _____

Signature _____ Day Phone _____

☐ **BILL ME:** *(U.S. institutional orders only. Purchase order required.)*

Purchase order # _____
Federal Tax ID 13559302 • GST 89102-8052

Name _____

Address _____

Phone _____ E-mail _____

Copy or detach page and send to: **John Wiley & Sons, One Montgomery Street, Suite 1000, San Francisco, CA 94104-4594**

Order Form can also be faxed to: **888-481-2665**

PROMO JBNND

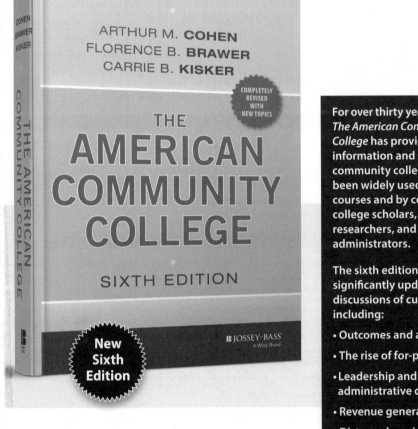

ARTHUR M. **COHEN**
FLORENCE B. **BRAWER**
CARRIE B. **KISKER**

COMPLETELY
REVISED
WITH
NEW TOPICS

THE

**AMERICAN
COMMUNITY
COLLEGE**

SIXTH EDITION

New
Sixth
Edition

JB JOSSEY-BASS
A Wiley Brand

For over thirty years, *The American Community College* has provided up-to-date information and statistics about community colleges. It has been widely used in graduate courses and by community college scholars, institutional researchers, and on-the-ground administrators.

The sixth edition has been significantly updated with discussions of current issues including:

• Outcomes and accountability

• The rise of for-profit colleges

• Leadership and administrative challenges

• Revenue generation

• Distance learning

The book concludes with a cogent response to contemporary criticisms of the institution.

JB JOSSEY-BASS
A Wiley Brand